UNDERSTANDING JAMES LEO HERLIHY

UNDERSTANDING CONTEMPORARY AMERICAN LITERATURE

Matthew J. Bruccoli, Founding Editor
Linda Wagner-Martin, Series Editor

Volumes on

Edward Albee | Sherman Alexie | Nelson Algren | Paul Auster
Nicholson Baker | John Barth | Donald Barthelme | The Beats
Thomas Berger | The Black Mountain Poets | Robert Bly
T. C. Boyle | Raymond Carver | Fred Chappell | Chicano Literature
Contemporary American Drama | Contemporary American Horror Fiction
Contemporary American Literary Theory
Contemporary American Science Fiction, 1926–1970
Contemporary American Science Fiction, 1970–2000
Contemporary Chicana Literature | Robert Coover | Philip K. Dick
James Dickey | E. L. Doctorow | Rita Dove | John Gardner | George Garrett
Tim Gautreaux | John Hawkes | Joseph Heller | Lillian Hellman | Beth Henley
James Leo Herlihy | John Irving | Randall Jarrell | Charles Johnson
Diane Johnson | Adrienne Kennedy | William Kennedy | Jack Kerouac
Jamaica Kincaid | Etheridge Knight | Tony Kushner | Ursula K. Le Guin
Denise Levertov | Bernard Malamud | David Mamet | Bobbie Ann Mason
Colum McCann | Cormac McCarthy | Jill McCorkle | Carson McCullers
W. S. Merwin | Arthur Miller | Lorrie Moore | Toni Morrison's Fiction
Vladimir Nabokov | Gloria Naylor | Joyce Carol Oates | Tim O'Brien
Flannery O'Connor | Cynthia Ozick | Walker Percy | Katherine Anne Porter
Richard Powers | Reynolds Price | Annie Proulx | Thomas Pynchon
Theodore Roethke | Philip Roth | May Sarton | Hubert Selby, Jr.
Mary Lee Settle | Neil Simon | Isaac Bashevis Singer | Jane Smiley
Gary Snyder | William Stafford | Robert Stone | Anne Tyler | Gerald Vizenor
Kurt Vonnegut | David Foster Wallace | Robert Penn Warren | James Welch
Eudora Welty | Tennessee Williams | August Wilson | Charles Wright

UNDERSTANDING

JAMES LEO HERLIHY

Robert Ward

The University of South Carolina Press

Published by the University of South Carolina Press
Columbia, South Carolina 29208

www.sc.edu/uscpress

Manufactured in the United States of America

21 20 19 18 17 16 15 14 13 12   10 9 8 7 6 5 4 3 2 1

Library of Congress Cataloging-in-Publication Data

Ward, Robert, 1966–
Understanding James Leo Herlihy / Robert Ward.
p. cm. — (Understanding contemporary American literature)
Includes bibliographical references and index.
ISBN 978-1-61117-074-0 (cloth : alk. paper)
1. Herlihy, James Leo—Criticism and interpretation. I. Title.
PS3515.E6325Z93 2012
812'.54—dc23

2011052856

This book was printed on a recycled paper with 30 percent postconsumer waste content.

Being a person was always more important than being a writer. I hope that my stories reflect that. I could be very happy thinking that they did.

James Leo Herlihy

CONTENTS

SERIES EDITOR'S PREFACE

The Understanding Contemporary American Literature series was founded by the estimable Matthew J. Bruccoli (1931–2008), who envisioned these volumes as guides or companions for students as well as good nonacademic readers, a legacy which will continue as new volumes are developed to fill in gaps among the nearly one hundred series volumes published to date and to embrace a host of new writers only now making their marks on our literature.

As Professor Bruccoli explained in his preface to the volumes he edited, because much influential contemporary literature makes special demands, "the word *understanding* in the titles was chosen deliberately. Many willing readers lack an adequate understanding of how contemporary literature works; that is, of what the author is attempting to express and the means by which it is conveyed." Aimed at fostering this understanding of good literature and good writers, the criticism and analysis in the series provide instruction in how to read certain contemporary writers—explicating their material, language, structures, themes, and perspectives—and facilitate a more profitable experience of the works under discussion.

In the twenty-first century Professor Bruccoli's prescience gives us an avenue to publish expert critiques of significant contemporary American writing. The series continues to map the literary landscape, and provide both instruction and enjoyment. Future volumes will seek to introduce new voices alongside canonized favorites, to chronicle the changing literature of our times, and to remain, as Prof. Bruccoli conceived, contemporary in the best sense of the word.

Linda Wagner-Martin, Series Editor

ACKNOWLEDGMENTS

I would first like to thank the University of Cumbria for the sabbatical that allowed me to start researching and writing this book. The sabbatical was partly spent at the University of Delaware's Special Collections, where the majority of Herlihy's papers are kept, and I am grateful for the kindness and patience the archivists showed me during my visit. Also deserving of my gratitude are the staff at the Howard Gotlieb Archival Research Center, Boston University, which houses another significant resource for scholars of Herlihy's work. Thanks also go to the following people: Cory McDonald, for granting me permission to use his wonderful photograph of Herlihy on the front cover of this book; Joe Frazier, for sharing the memories of his friendship with Herlihy; and Steve Longstaffe and Penny Bradshaw, for always supporting the idea of the book with enthusiasm.

The book owes much to the comradeship of close friends in the UK, their humor, their generosity of spirit. I won't mention you by name because you know who you are, and I miss you very much. Since moving from Britain to the USA, I have also been fortunate in meeting people who have become good friends and have helped take my mind off the book with the temptation of nice meals, civilized conversation, wine. And finally I thank my wife, Suzannah Camm, who has given me the time and space to finish this book, without ever allowing it to compromise the loving relationship we have. She has read and listened to numerous drafts of each chapter and offered advice where it was plainly needed. Any errors the reader finds, though, are mine alone.

CHAPTER 1

Understanding James Leo Herlihy

Leo Herlihy was born on 27 February 1927 in Detroit, Michigan, to parents of German and Irish heritage. His father, a construction engineer, and mother, a housewife, brought up their five children to believe in Roman Catholicism, traditional marriage, and the importance of working-class labor. From a young age Herlihy sought alternatives to such a predetermined life. His sister Jean introduced her younger brother to the literature of Thomas Wolfe, Upton Sinclair, F. Scott Fitzgerald, and others from the Book-of-the-Month Club. "As soon as I found out words," remembers Herlihy, "I knew I wanted to write." In 1934 at age seven he received a Dial typewriter as a Christmas present and began composing scripts for his own puppet shows. When he became an adolescent, the family and the city seemed insurmountable barriers to another, more artistic life: "How could anybody growing up on 76th South Sugar Street, Detroit, be a writer?"[1] The tensions between parents and children frequently appear in his writing, though Detroit is often supplanted by the faraway environments of Florida, New York, and Los Angeles inhabited by his characters.

World War II provided the catalyst for which Herlihy was searching. At the age of eighteen in 1945 he joined the U.S. Navy, though he was never to see active duty.[2] In the service he met John Lyons, an English professor from Loyola University, Chicago. Lyons quickly became a friend and mentor, helping Herlihy develop an appreciation for literature, especially short stories and plays—the forms he would go on to master in his writing. As his term in the navy was nearing its end, Herlihy had no wish to return to his family. Instead he wanted an education, one that taught him how to write. Knowing that his friend lacked formal entrance qualifications and disliked "play[ing] by the rules," Lyons suggested Black Mountain College, a small and remote learning community then situated on the banks of Lake Eden, North Carolina.[3]

Opening in the fall of 1933, Black Mountain was certainly an extraordinary place. To its founder, John Andrew Rice, an artistic education was fundamental to the intellectual health of the individual and society. However, an education at the college was not the only learning offered there. "Most important to one's growth," wrote Annie Albers, "is to see oneself leave the safe ground of accepted conventions and to find oneself alone and self-dependent. It is an adventure which can permeate one's whole being."[4] By 1946, as Herlihy faced the possibility of having to move back in with his parents, the college seemed the perfect place for him to spend his GI Bill funding. After his application was rejected, he traveled to the college to confront the person responsible for admitting students: "'How come you turned me down? I'm just what you need': And so they looked me over and they said, 'Well, indeed you are. Come in September.'"[5]

For Herlihy, Black Mountain College was a "wonderful situation."[6] The desire to learn everything from the start—writing, painting, acting, psychology—led him to enroll in eleven courses at once, a route that his adviser attempted to dissuade him from taking. Here between 1946 and 1948 he would meet lifelong friends and important influences on his growth as a creative person. The poet M. C. Richards gave clear advice on improving his prose style, advice that he both respected and used. Richards and Herlihy liked each other from the start, and they continued their friendship through correspondence up until his death in 1993.

Similarly, Lyle Bongé, with whom Herlihy shared a dorm, became a close friend and influence. Bongé's photography recorded Mardi Gras and the grotesquery of everyday experience, a focus that dominates much of Herlihy's writing.[7] As with Richards, Herlihy kept their friendship alive through correspondence, punctuated by the occasional visit. The letters, now housed in the University of Delaware's Special Collections, are beautifully crafted documents, fragments of a life that are invaluable for our understanding of a writer who has been unjustly missing critical and biographical attention.[8]

Toward the end of 1947 Anaïs Nin came to the college on a four-day visit. At the time Nin was a diarist, avant-garde artist, and model. Her visit, as Herlihy remembers, "was just the most glamorous thing that ever happened to me . . . and I didn't take my eyes off her the whole time."[9] They were to become intimate friends, she referring to him as "my spiritual son."[10] In an interview conducted over twenty years later, Herlihy vividly recalled the influence that Nin's visit had on him as a fledgling writer:

> One of the things she asked me was what I hoped to do with my writing. I said I hoped I could write a novel—I was strongly under the influence of Upton Sinclair's *The Jungle*—and I hoped I could write a novel . . . that would make people feel how treacherous and sad it was . . . that we all have such suffering in our lives. If we could just feel the suffering and somehow affect it and cause people to be more concerned with the idea of maybe making less of it. That was my ambition. She said that seemed like a really good idea. And I said, "What do you do? What do you do with your writing?" She said: "I want to contribute to the world one fulfilled person—myself." And that was like the beginning of—for me—a life-long double-mindedness. There was this part of me that wanted to do something for the world and part of me that wanted to understand what it meant to be a fulfilled individual. More and more I've realized that Anaïs was making a terribly important point that was never really understood by a great mass of people until the nineteen-sixties and then more and more in the seventies and eighties. People didn't understand that one can't really have a profound effect on others without *being* someone—the effect that you have on others comes from who you are. Anaïs understood this. I think she was the first person I ever encountered in my life who really understood that the great art form of the Twentieth Century is the Art of the Person. That, if you want to affect the world you live in, first of all you have to affect yourself, you have to affect the kind of being that you really think the world should be populated with. And that's what Anaïs did. It was the central and strongest and most enduring influence on me and I'm very grateful for it.[11]

With Nin's departure the experimental artistic atmosphere at Black Mountain began to seem stifling. Herlihy's desire to learn how to write clearly was frowned upon, the artistic equivalent of drawing the perfect circle. As a result he kept much of his writing private, asking only trusted friends such as Richards and Bongé for advice. The critic Isaac Rosenfeld, then teaching creative writing at the college, disliked Herlihy's short stories intensely and encouraged his student to take an aptitude test to discover what else he could do with his life. Herlihy listened: the test told him to be a writer. The second vocation on the list was acting, about which Herlihy was equally as passionate.[12] He decided to leave the college and spent some time hitchhiking across the country before becoming a student at Pasadena Playhouse from 1948 to 1950.

The experience at Pasadena allowed Herlihy to grow artistically. His dislike of many of the theatrical roles he was given prompted him to return to writing in the hope of creating more suitable characters. As a result *Streetlight*

Sonata: A Modern Tragedy was performed at the Pasadena Playhouse in 1950. Directed by Philip van Dyke and John Landreth, the play reproduced "a skid row dream street where people stand around waiting for their dreams to become the whole show." Three years later *Moon in Capricorn* was produced in an Off-Broadway theater in New York.[13] *Moon in Capricorn* is set in the astrologer Madame Zoe's apartment, where the audience is introduced to Jeanne Wilkes. Wilkes lives only for her own pleasure, an attitude that her contemporary society is unable to tolerate. Both plays received only limited, localized attention. Despite becoming RCA Fellow at Yale Drama School in 1956, Herlihy drifted into a series of dead-end jobs.[14] According to her diaries, Nin was concerned about her friend and encouraged him to move to New York, a city that she hoped would act as muse to his creative development. However, life on the social and economic periphery was perhaps the inspiration for which Herlihy was searching. Here was a world, on the edge both physically and psychologically, where many of his characters would wind up.

Herlihy became a recognized playwright in 1958 with the successful run on Broadway of *Blue Denim,* which he wrote in collaboration with William "Bill" Noble, a drama instructor at Pasadena Playhouse.[15] The play, the plot of which looks through the keyhole of a postwar suburban home, received notoriety as one of the first pieces of drama to use a comfortable middle-class family to expose the issue of teenage sex and the perils of back-street abortions. Herlihy's entrance into the realm of successful writers seemed sealed when the play was adapted to film by Philip Dunne and starred Brandon de Wilde and Carol Lynley. However, Dunne's movie obscured Herlihy's role as the original writer, as did other adaptations of his work. In the end he, like the characters who populate his work, was fated to remain on the fringes of American letters.

The concern with breaking down the image of the suburban middle-class family is one that also dominates his first novel, *All Fall Down,* published in 1960.[16] Like those of the Bartleys in *Blue Denim,* the lives of the Williams family are shaped by the tension between material comfort and emotional insecurity. However, *All Fall Down* pushes that tension further, establishing Herlihy's interest in the psychology of his characters. Like much of Herlihy's work that came after, there are two important ways that this psychology is brought to the surface: the first is through dreams; the second is through a gothic landscape that invades the everyday reality of Herlihy's fictional world.

In the only sustained, though unpublished, critical study of Herlihy, Jayne D. Mack devotes herself to the dream motif in his work. She has found that these sleeping dreams and daydreams have a particular structure. First, there are dreams that expose a specific problem that results from tensions within the family. In most cases these dreams are experienced by adolescent characters with overbearing mothers, such as Clinton Williams in *All Fall Down,* Gloria Random in *The Season of the Witch* (1971), Rudy Filbertson in "The Sleep of Baby Filbertson" (1959), and though somewhat older, Joe Buck in *Midnight Cowboy* (1965). These initial dreams often enable the characters to begin to understand their present situations and map paths to maturity. As Mack suggests, "problem dreams become solution dreams," and that pattern is a key device that originates in Herlihy himself: "I have always had a very active dream life, have recorded thousands of them in note-books over the years. . . . And being a dreamer myself, I seem to write of characters who dream. At first, I tried to eliminate the dreams because I was told no one wanted to read them; but soon discovered they were essential."[17]

These so-called problem dreams also contribute to Herlihy's representation of a gothic environment. This inspiration comes from the peculiarities of the southern gothic, at least as that term pertains to Herlihy's reading of Carson McCullers and Flannery O'Connor. Like theirs, his suburban and urban environments become nightmarish, moonlit, shrouded in fog. In this setting his characters cast shadows on the dark ground, and their faces take on grotesque distortions, like the caricatures in the photography of Bongé and Stephen Arnold.[18] As Mack says, this setting is sometimes temporary, as Herlihy cares too much for his characters simply to abandon them. It needs to be noted, though, that when older characters dream, such as Mary Ellen McClure in *A Story That Ends with a Scream and Eight Others* (1967), the gothic landscape, the grotesque existence of their everyday lives, is reinforced.

Sexuality is another major theme, which dreams often expose in Herlihy's work. His characters struggle coming to terms with themselves as sexual beings, at times resulting in sexual dreams becoming incestuous. As Herlihy was a gay man who spent his early life trying to understand and articulate his own sexuality, it may be useful to consider a latent homosexuality as part of this struggle. There is little evidence of this latency in some early characters, though Clinton Williams does fall in love with the masculine femme fatal Echo O'Brien, but we see it very much on the surface of later work, especially the short story "Miguel" (1959) and perhaps Herlihy's masterpiece, *Midnight Cowboy.*

That novel started germinating in Herlihy's imagination as early as 1963, "when the character of Joe Buck started waltzing around inside my head, saying little things to me, being there when I closed my eyes."[19] Joe moves from small-town life to Manhattan to make his fortune dressed as a cowboy stud. His childlike naivety allows Herlihy to present him as an unknowingly gay icon, one who seeks rich women but ends up being picked up by confused and lonely men who are obsessed with their mothers. Herlihy refuses to abandon his protagonist to this existence, pushing him instead into a very human and loving friendship with the trickster Rico Rizzo, perhaps the most vivid character in all of Herlihy's works.

His work had long been courted by Hollywood, and *Midnight Cowboy* was no exception. John Schlesinger's film of the same title starred Dustin Hoffman as Rico and John Voight as Joe. Perhaps in order to be accepted in mainstream cinema, the film portrays Joe as a homosexual virgin, though it retains the novel's sexual motifs and subtexts. The film earned three Academy Awards (for best director, best picture, and best screenplay by Waldo Salt), the first X-rated movie to do so. The movie has justifiably gained a popular and critical reputation as a masterpiece of cinema during the 1960s, though its original precursor, the novel, has been largely forgotten and, at the time of writing this introduction, remains out of print.

The success of the movie gave Herlihy much-needed financial security. It allowed him to keep his apartment in New York as well as buy a beautiful home in Key West, Florida, a region that was often the setting of his work. He also noted a falseness in the way many people started to talk to him, and the unnecessary attention left him with doubts about his future as a writer. As he noted in a letter to M. C. Richards in 1970: "There's something else disturbing going on in my life. . . . *Midnight Cowboy* has made me too well known for my comfort and has put some things off balance." He continued: "I'm not writing well and this offends my vanity, and yet I'm writing well enough to know I have to continue. I do hope and pray that after this book I will be delivered forever from the horrors of fiction writing."[20] The book referred to, which is almost certainly *The Season of the Witch,* would be Herlihy's final novel.

The Season of the Witch marks Herlihy's growth as a political writer.[21] The novel retains the psychological and emotional concerns that are so evident in the earlier work. But Herlihy had become tired of simply "reviewing the pain" of his characters. Instead he wanted a novel that reflected the momentous transformation in culture that the 1960s represented and to "suggest a philosophical approach that would be useful."[22] He saw the hippy movement as a salvation for America, and always the "chronic hitchhiker,"[23] as Nin called him, he took off on a road trip with his friend Evan Rhodes to document the new phenomenon.[24] He witnessed "holes of cultural experimentation" that could "bring forth new cities."[25] It represented a new age, one by which he felt reborn and invigorated. He would take part in stop-the-war protests and the attempt to elevate the White House by holding hands and meditation, and on a whim he would purchase one hundred copies of Howard Zinn's anti-Vietnam book *The Logic of Withdrawal* (1967) to give to friends. *The Season of the Witch* (1971) can be understood only in those personal and social contexts.

Like much of Herlihy's writing, *The Season of the Witch* is based on a tension between mother and child. In running away from her comfortable middle-class home, the protagonist, Gloria Random, a female Huckleberry Finn, is casting off the shackles of the past and reinventing herself in a new and exhilarating context. Her journey can be read as the genesis of a golden age: "We'll learn to be *aware,* we'll learn to watch ourselves in such a way that when the ghosts of our parents show themselves in our behavior, we'll be free to pick and choose. We'll take what's wise and beautiful, and be happy that it's a part of us, and we'll simply reject what's ugly and dark."[26] As such, Gloria's journey and philosophy represent an autobiographical fragment of her creator.

As the above letter to Richards shows, Herlihy's love of writing had become strained. He enjoyed his involvement in the peace movement, campaigning for gay rights, and traveling to Spain, Morocco, and South America. At his home in Key West, and later in Los Angeles, he enjoyed socializing with friends, such as Tennessee Williams and Christopher Isherwood. He enjoyed gardening and cooking and anticipating his annual shipment of wine freshly harvested from the vineyards of Italy. He enjoyed teaching writing at City College, New York, where he hoped to give "less of myself and more of an availability."[27] He felt that writers shut themselves away like monks, and Herlihy no longer desired a self-imposed exile. However, as Bongé said, "even though he gave up writing—he was very much still a letter writer. He wrote to me constantly. There was never more than a sentence about current affairs in a letter of five pages. It was all very personal and intimate. About sex and death but also about his joys, and not much about sorrow; on working on his garden, on cooking, with often a whole page devoted to a supper he had had the night before; how he had fixed the meal; something new that he had learnt."[28]

Herlihy was certainly hurt by the lack of critical attention accorded his work.[29] But as much as there was a need to give up writing, there was also a compulsion to continue. Such tension is evident in a letter written to Richards in 1973: "I'm trying to stage a reconciliation with the typewriter with which machine I've been on the outs for some years, and it is an uphill path."[30] Even so, no more of his work would be published. Three of Herlihy's short plays were performed Off Broadway between 1965 and 1973, and their collective title upon publication, *Stop, You're Killing Me* (1970), certainly reflected the mood of the author. One of those plays, *Terrible Jim Fitch*—a story of a pimp and a prostitute in a motel room outside Albuquerque, New Mexico—was screened on BBC's Thirty Minute Theatre in 1971 and starred Nicol Williamson and Marianne Faithful. Despite the respect the performance earned from reviewers, *Stop, You're Killing Me* marked the end of Herlihy's vocation as a published playwright.

He had become instead what Nin had called a self-fulfilled person; cooking, teaching, and gardening had become extensions of his creativity, not an end to it. "The garden here is terrific," Herlihy wrote beautifully to Richards in the winter of 1974; "the tomatoes have flowers on them. The lettuce has been thinned out. The swiss chard is healthy. The beans and peas have begun to climb the maze of rainbow yarn on the fence, the sunflowers are a foot tall already, the cauliflower and broccoli are growing by leaps and bounds, the bell peppers are holding their own, the zinnies [*sic*] and marigolds have appeared."[31]

As the 1980s began, Herlihy's literary reputation faded from view, occasionally interrupted with letters from readers and interviews in gay magazines.[32] For Herlihy, the decade of the 1980s was not a good time. AIDS had ravaged the gay community, killing close friends and acquaintances. Getting older also brought its familiar problems. By the end of the decade he suffered from constant pain in his teeth and also in his shoulder, had a kidney stone, had been diagnosed with a weak heart, and was taking medication to ward off a stroke. After his friend James Kirkwood, the writer, died of cancer in the spring of 1989, Herlihy's depression, which had long affected him, became more acute.[33] As he wrote to Bongé in the summer of that year, "I think that business of dying 'conscious and in control' is all well and good, and I hope it for me, too. But shit, what's the alternative? A bullet, a la Hemingway with brains all over the wallpaper. I mean if you (one) decides to end it all, what's better than going to sleep and waking up in the new place."[34]

Herlihy committed suicide on 21 October 1993, aged sixty-six, by taking an overdose of sleeping pills at his home in Los Angeles. After the funeral a young man, perhaps a friend or reader, was seen "huddled all night on the kerb in front of the house." As the obituary continued, "In life Herlihy took in and helped many of the misfit types who people his novels and plays; he often filled his home with them and protected them from the police."[35] The personal engagement with his subject is a crucial part of understanding his overall aesthetic. Though born in what Herlihy referred to as the dark ages, his body of work is a product of what he liked to term the "golden age" of the 1950s and 1960s, reaching its conclusion with the eventual disillusionment of the period.[36]

CHAPTER 2

Blue Denim

In the fall of 1954 Anaïs Nin wrote in her diary, "Jim going through a difficult period. His novelette unpublished, his novel unpublished, and his job at 'Paper Plates' brings him just enough for rent and food (and a paper plate regime for all his friends)."[1] Four years later, though, Herlihy had finished his RCA fellowship at Yale Drama School, and his play *Crazy October* (1958), starring the notorious Tallulah Bankhead, was in rehearsals. Herlihy had written other plays during the early part of the decade, including *Streetlight Sonata* (1950) and *Moon in Capricorn* (1953), but it was not until the opening of *Blue Denim* on Broadway in 1958 that he began to attract acclaim from reviewers and publishers.[2] It is, said one reviewer, "one of the best plays of the season . . . present[ing] a notable portrait of unnotable people."[3]

The play, written in collaboration with William Noble, focuses on the Bartleys, an ordinary middle-class family who live in the suburbs of Detroit.[4] An opening tableau shows the family sitting around the dining table: the father, a retired army major, who performs his role as head of house; his wife, Jessie, a forty-something homemaker; Lillian, an unmarried daughter in her early twenties; and a teenager called Arthur. They represent a stereotype of the prosperous family at midcentury as pictured in popular TV shows such as *Father Knows Best* and in magazines such as *American Life*. The domestic home was an almost-sacred commodity as it gave a sense of moral rightness and security to a country beset by the anxieties of cold-war life. *Blue Denim,* as an issue-based drama, cuts through the veneer of this familial portrait in order to expose a controversial hidden world of teenage rebellion, underage sex, and illegal abortion.

As an exposé of domestic life, *Blue Denim* was not on its own. Arthur Miller's *Death of a Salesman* (1949), for instance, shows the emotional breakdown and tragedy at the heart of the domestic home; Tennessee Williams's *Cat on a Hot Tin Roof* (1955) presents family as a cover for guilt, unrealized hopes, and suppressed sexualities; Lorraine Hansberry's *A Raisin in the Sun* (1959) finds an African American familial need of upward mobility and freedom thwarted by white prejudice. Narratives of teenage unruliness also became a national obsession. Perhaps Holden Caulfield, the adolescent narrator of J. D. Salinger's novel *The Catcher in the Rye* (1951), captures this best through his depiction of the growing alienation between parents and their children. In cinemas *Rebel without a Cause* (1955) and *The Wild One* (1953) diagnosed the same generational rift and juxtaposed concerned adults alongside juvenile delinquents. The 1950s, then, was a context fractured by two conflicting worlds: one that included the family as the epitome of American idealism; and the other that rebelled against it. *Blue Denim* must be understood in this context.

In *Homeward Bound: American Families in the Cold War,* Elaine Tyler May uses the word "containment" to define everyday life in the typical middle-class home. The idea was an important part of anticommunist politics during the 1950s, which used trials organized by the House Un-American Activities Committee and an atmosphere of suspicion and paranoia whipped up by Senator Joseph R. McCarthy to root out opponents of capitalism. May refers to a "domestic version" of that idea: "The sphere of influence was the home. Within its walls, potentially dangerous social forces of the new age might be tamed."[5] This anesthetic quality of suburban family life is subtly invested in a description of the Bartleys' dining room: "The dining room, upstairs, seems cozy, but cluttered and overheated. . . . The furnishings might have been selected from *Saturday Evening Post:* the large round table with four chairs, the buffet against the wall, the tea wagon for whiskey decanters and glasses, and a comfortable chaise longue [*sic*] within easy reach of the telephone stand. A chandelier hangs over the dining-room table and there are framed prints on the walls—a too familiar Van Gogh and smaller still-life floral studies" (3).

Like Henrik Ibsen's sets of heavily furnished rooms, used in *A Doll's House* (1879) to convey the docility and claustrophobia of characters' lives, the Bartleys' dining room is cluttered but tidy. The room is clearly the product of a daily habit of cleaning and ordering that reflects the parents' own regulated (she folding stockings, he filling out check stubs) lives. Indeed the room seems too warm for anything except eating and sleeping. This direction allows us to understand the Major, who appears as if "he has spent too much of his life sleeping," and Jessie, who is also "a little-tired looking" (4). These are no minor details; they use character to allude to a wider social sensibility. "The Sleepwalkers' Children" was the original title of the play.[6] Herlihy believed that a section of the postwar population was in a state of slumber over controversial issues that affected relationships with their children, which they did not want to face. *Blue Denim* was written for that population.

An awareness of the organization of the stage helps us to understand how Herlihy confronted his audiences with those issues. Joshua Logan's Broadway production of *Blue Denim,* for instance, remained faithful to the original script and made the dining room and basement the center points of the performance. If the dining room signifies routine and order, the basement is designed to have the opposite effect. Rather than neatness and comfort, we see furnishings that are "rickety" and "broken," the decor is of "concrete block," and there are several "abandoned toys" and an "old day bed" on the floor (3). As in many suburban homes, the Bartleys use this space as storage, but the Major also allows it to be used as a space for Arthur and his friend Ernie to study. For fifteen-year-old Arthur, however, it is also a "refuge" (3): "Arthur flips the light switch at the top of the stairs, illuminating the basement area. Now the two boys work in almost military unison—obviously this is routine. Arthur drags a cardboard box from under the stairs and brings out the following: poker chips, cards, cigarets, matches, a bottle opener and paper cups. Meanwhile Ernie places his books on the cot and, from under his coat takes the quart of beer pilfered from the icebox and places it at the center of the table. He lights two cigarets. They are now two men of the world with a vengeance" (16). The closing words, "with a vengeance," directed the actors Burt Brinckerhoff (Arthur) and Warren Berlinger (Ernie) in a performance clearly designed to shock a Broadway middle-class audience. Thus the play taps into a pressing social question of the age: "Parents! Do you know what your children are doing?"

Both the Major and Jessie think they can answer that question, though they seem to have little idea what their son and his friends are doing. As if drinking, gambling, smoking, and theft were not enough to shock, we are introduced to Janet Willard, who will be central to the play's main plot. Janet is an "attractive girl of sixteen," a girlfriend of Arthur's, and she enters the basement from a side door adjacent to the yard (22). Clearly a regular in the basement, she on this particular visit asks Ernie to forge a sick note so that she can miss school and go shopping with her sister Norma instead. After Ernie leaves, the atmosphere in the basement changes dramatically.

Arthur is more honest, Janet is more emotional, and the scene quickly becomes intimate.

By the end of act 1 the audience is left with no doubt that both teenagers have had sex—though this certainty relies more on suggestion as explicit details remained too controversial to dramatize on the Broadway stage. Even so, things were changing in 1958. As McCarthyism faded into the past and the decade was on the cusp of the 1960s, there existed what David Allyn calls "growing public demand for open discussion about sexual issues."[7] The shock of Janet's pregnancy, announced in act 2, and Arthur's plans for an abortion serve to engage a contemporary audience in that discussion. Consider, for example, the following piece of dialogue, which shows Arthur trying to persuade his friend to help arrange an abortion for Janet:

ERNIE: Look, I'm not trying to scare the hell out of you or anything, but . . . well,—like I said before—it's murder.
ARTHUR: Don't keep saying that. We didn't mean it to be a baby. It was just her and me Ernie, we didn't think! Besides, it hasn't even got a heart or a name yet. It's just trouble. Not a person.
ERNIE: It's alive isn't it? (52)

The difference of opinion reflects the two main positions of the proabortion/antiabortion debate that would evolve into a more direct confrontation between traditional values and women's rights in the proceeding years. However, the action of the play does not focus on taking sides. Rather it highlights the desperate circumstances that lead young women to seek abortions and the unregulated and illegal back-street clinics that perform them. As Ernie says: "Listen, Art, these operations are dangerous. I mean the doctors that do it aren't so hot sometimes. That's why they get kicked out of the profession, 'cause they weren't very ethical to start with" (52).

Even though Ernie cannot use the word "abortion" on the Broadway stage ("terrible operation" was acceptable[8]), his words are telling. Although abortion was technically legal, most doctors sanctioned only "therapeutic" termination, in order to protect the health of the mother. After the war, as demand for the procedure grew, many hospitals established abortion committees that considered requests from pregnant women. In the rare cases where permission was granted, many women were made to sign a form agreeing to their sterilization. These barriers helped fuel a thriving back-street industry, which was responsible for up to a million abortions each year. According to May, "as many as 90 percent of premarital pregnancies were aborted" by an industry "responsible for an estimated 40 percent of all maternal deaths."[9] Politicians seldom broached the issue, and families lacked the confidence and knowledge to discuss it with their children. For desperate young women such as Janet, to whom could they turn? To whom could they speak for advice and support?

For most Americans, the back-street abortion clinic was a "secret world." One heard about it and gained access to it via rumor and hearsay. For some girls who could not afford the fees or were too afraid to go through with the operation, pregnancy and giving their babies up for adoption must have seemed the only choices. In *Abortion Wars: A Half Century of Struggle, 1950–2000,* Rickie Solinger exposes a fate even worse than that: "After World War II tens of thousands of white girls and women who became pregnant outside of marriage each year were unable to determine either the course of their pregnancies or the conditions of their maternity. They were, in astonishing numbers, deeply shamed by their families, removed from school, diagnosed as psychologically disturbed, and defined as non-mothers without husbands."[10] Although Janet carries only a vague sense of these possibilities, she does recognize the dangers and pleads with Arthur for an alternative course of action, such as marriage. But the decision seems to be taken out of her hands by Arthur, who has failed in his attempt to speak with his parents.

Despite arranging the abortion, Ernie develops into a wise and maturing protagonist. It is he who urges Arthur to speak to his parents. As a result Arthur ascends the stairs to the dining room, and the following scene takes place:

ARTHUR: Mom, I want to talk to you.
JESSIE: Your father's been at it ever since dinner. Simply because I exceeded my July budget by a penny or two!
ARTHUR: (*Interrupting*) Mom, you and me can talk, can't we?
JESSIE: Why, of course. We always could. (*Suddenly aware of his appearance*) Arthur! Have you been fighting? You're filthy! How many days have you worn that shirt?
ARTHUR: Shirt? What difference does it . . . Mom! I said I had to talk to you! It's important!
JESSIE: What difference? I'm trying to get the laundry together! Can you co-operate?
ARTHUR: Mom, will you shut up!

(Major *enters from the living room, carrying a large checkbook, which he places on the table*)

MAJOR: Who are you telling to shut up?
JESSIE: That was intended for his mother?

MAJOR: What's wrong with him?
ARTHUR: Nothing. You know how mother gets!
JESSIE: How *does* mother get?
ARTHUR: I just said I wanted to talk to her.
MAJOR: When you talk to people you don't start in by being rude. Now, what is it?
JESSIE: Yes, what is it?
ARTHUR: Well, it's . . . uh . . .
MAJOR: Nothing serious I hope.

(*His parents sit facing him.* Arthur *looks from one to the other, disgusted with the futility of even trying to speak*)

ARTHUR: Oh, crap! (54–55)

The encounter is revealing in a number of ways as the issues of underage sex, pregnancy, and abortion are woven into problems of communication in the family. Arthur cannot seem to find the words to speak to his parents. There is interruption after interruption, but the essential message is littered with deviations and sidetracked by petty squabbles.

It is understandable that an audience might see such scenes as comic, especially relating to the old-fashioned naivety of the father and the domestic fussiness ("Can't you ever break something that isn't part of a set") of the mother (67).[11] Such stereotypes of bumbling parents could be found in the numerous Saturday night TV and radio sitcoms of the time. However, the humor in *Blue Denim* is not an end in itself but more of a temporary comic relief in the serious drama unfolding. There was a similar breakdown of communication between parents and their teenagers in other cultural narratives of the 1950s, and the relationship between these texts is far from accidental. Indeed many writers continued to employ realism in order to open a window onto the world of the contemporary family. *Death of a Salesman* is a now-classic example of that domestic world torn apart, among other things, by the inability of every family member to respond openly and honestly to each other. Willy and the Major share a dream of their sons becoming executives in successful corporations. Biff and Arthur simply want to work on a farm. Where Biff has shamed his parents by doing time in jail, Arthur is about to do the same when the news of the abortion finally leaks out.

Brooks Atkinson, in one of the earliest and most astute reviews of the Broadway production of *Blue Denim*, may be correct in his view that "the distance is too great. You cannot talk until the most harrowing part of the trouble has ended."[12] But we should not forget the play's impulse to present the other side of the story:

ARTHUR: I'll say it again and again! They wouldn't help me. Neither of them! They wouldn't even listen to me!
ERNIE: You never gave them a chance. You went up there and all you said was "Er" and "Ah" and "Dad, I want to talk to you." Did you once say, "Dad, I'm in trouble"? Did you say that? (78)

That balanced narrative approach serves to engage and not alienate a middle-class theatergoing audience. The strength of *Blue Denim* lies in just that. It is not enough to confront and accuse, as all the family members have their faults and all need to address the problem. But that, as Atkinson states, is left to the end of the play. For now, instead of confronting his parents about the situation, Arthur steals a check from the dining room and forges his father's signature. The stolen money—ninety-two dollars—contributes to the cost of Janet's abortion.

In American theater, though, the pigeons often come home to roost. The Major finds out about the stolen check in act 3. In an effort to regain a sense of authority over the home, and prompted by Jessie's comment that "you and Arthur are perfect strangers," the Major pleads with his son to "pour it right out" and "we're going to listen quietly" (88). This is the first time in the play that the Major has tried to have an intimate conversation with Arthur. However, the meeting does not go according to the Major's plan. In line with the father-son dialogue dramatized in key plays of the period—Willy Loman's tense moments with Biff in *Death of a Salesman,* for instance, or Big Daddy's attempt at truth with Brick in *Cat on a Hot Tin Roof*—the conversation serves only to widen a sense of division between the two characters. Reminded by Jessie to keep his temper under control, the Major nevertheless turns a family conversation into a military-style interrogation filled with accusations and threats of violence: "You're flirting with a cyclone. When I get done with you, they won't put you in jail . . . they'll put you in a hospital! See?" Arthur's reaction—"I hate you! I hate this whole goddam family!"—brings the crisis to a head, and when the truth of Janet's abortion is finally revealed by Lillian, it forces the family to wake from its slumber and begin to adopt a more honest exploration of their relationships with each other (93, 97).

After she overhears a telephone conversation between Arthur and Ernie, Lillian tells her parents the news of Janet's abortion. The horror and anxiety at the news, though, quickly give way to the promise of resolution. The Major, for the first time, cries, exposing a humanity that will invest his plan to reach out to his son. That plan involves a meal and coffee, brought to the table by Jessie and Lillian, and sitting for a few hours talking about other things. Arthur also has a newfound hope, in his resolve to Janet that "I'm going to work this thing out" (109). In this light we can understand the closing scene of the play:

(The Major *seats himself at the head of the table.* Arthur, *meanwhile, closes the cellar door, shooting the bolt home with finality. Then he takes one last long look around, as if saying goodbye to the basement and all that it represents . . .*)

ARTHUR: "Dad, can you and me talk for a minute?" (110)

Arthur's leaving the basement for the last time may be an indication that fractures and divisions within the Bartley household are over. But the play ends on a hope rather than an actuality of resolution, reflecting perhaps what John Gassner calls "Broadway's optimism and penchant for reformation of character."[13]

The loser in this possibility of a happy ending, of course, is Janet. To understand the development of this character, we need to revisit the above scene where the Major broaches the subject of the stolen check with Arthur. Here the father-son dialogue represents a patriarchal space where the voice of the female is policed and censored. Intimate family conversations that silence the mother figure pattern throughout postwar American drama. As David Savran suggests in his analysis of the era's theater, "Women are associated with a chaotic and disruptive natural realm that must be subjugated and rigorously controlled so that it cannot undermine the three cardinal masculine characteristics: achievement, responsibility, and authority."[14] In this light we can easily see the Major's insistence that Jessie "keep still" (92) in line with Big Daddy's exclusion of Big Mamma in his moment of truth with his son Brick, or Willy Loman's insistence that his wife Linda keep out of his conversation with Biff.

Extending the private father-son dialogue to reflect what Robert Vorlicky calls a "social dialogue . . . determined by a male masculine ethos" helps us to understand the subtext of these plays.[15] Indeed family drama offered an ideal terrain to explore the postwar condition of American ideas of freedom and social justice as they related to the experiences of gender and sexual minorities. It is a "masculine ethos" that seems to enable the Major to understand and deal with the consequences of his son's behavior. Where underage sex affirms Arthur's transition from adolescence to manhood (a fact reinforced by the Major's "man-to-man" talk at the end of the play), it serves only to reduce Janet to the status of a juvenile delinquent. As Douglas Miller argues: "Perceptions of female delinquency themselves reveal much more about mainstream attitudes towards rebellion. In the fifties, delinquent boys' crimes were wholly those of property or violence. The twenty percent of delinquents who were female, in contrast, got in trouble usually for crimes pertaining to sex or autonomy. Nearly always, a girl was considered delinquent for running away from home or participating in a mutually acquiescent sex act. . . . Many such girls were sent to state institutions (reform schools)."[16]

As is the case for Esther in Sylvia Plath's semi-autobiographical novel *The Bell Jar* (1963), the possibility of reform school is yet another pressure for Janet to carry. The mark of delinquency has also clouded her sense of a future. As she stands in the basement, Arthur attempts to block any details of the abortion ("Don't! Don't, Jan, please!), preferring instead to reenact the original sex act. Janet is horrified and appears a less-confident figure; she "*shudders, swaying with revulsion*" at the thought of what has happened to her (107).

In addressing issues of female delinquency, the character Lillian offers an interesting counterpoint to Janet. Lillian's relationship with Gilbert Sorenson is surrounded by secrecy. There is a hint, for instance, that they may be engaged, as Lillian is wearing a ring. Gilbert is never brought to the house to meet the parents, and we learn from Ernie that he could be associated with criminal activities. The relationship ends when Lillian comes home one evening with a black eye and a "mussed up" appearance. Although parents encouraged their daughters to date different boys and even go steady, the etiquette of dating allowed petting but certainly no sex before marriage. Gilbert has clearly overstepped the mark and receives a slap on the face for his nerve. Rather than appear horrified at the assault on her daughter, Jessie sees the black eye as a symbol of virtue. As she says, "Throughout the entire episode, I have felt nothing but pride. You have conducted yourself beautifully" (60).

Herlihy went on to develop in his work a preoccupation with bringing together protagonists who differ in terms of their ethnicity, sexuality, social background, or appearance. There are numerous examples: Berry-Berry and Kitty Twist in *All Fall Down* (1960); Joe Buck and Rico Rizzo in *Midnight Cowboy* (1965); and Gloria and Peter in *The Season of the Witch* (1971), to name but a few. Lillian, who has resisted sexual advances, and Janet, who has not, also make an interesting pair as they represent apparently antithetical experiences of female behavior. But even though these characters are constructed as opposites in Jessie's mind, we are still made to see them in a similar light. In this scene the draught caused by the yard door being opened by

Janet, who has come to see Arthur before her operation, brings Lillian down into the basement: "Lillian *opens the cellar door with a rattle of the knob.* Janet *hides in the shadows as* Lillian *descends the steps.* Lillian *stops abruptly in the center of the basement, staring disbelievingly at the closed hatch*" (72). The scene relies on the strength of the direction and acting, but it has the potential to be one of the most poignant moments of the play. In a dimly lit and quiet scene, we watch Janet watching Lillian. What seems a portrait of conflicting values (as conflicting perhaps as the laughing woman and Linda Loman in *Death of a Salesman*) can also be considered as one character representing almost a mirror image of the other character. The relationship between the two is unspoken because it lacks any power in the home to articulate it, but its silence could be read as exposing the construction of female archetypes by a postwar "domestic imagination."[17]

Such a reading of the play's more symbolic moments helps expand a particular point made in Atkinson's review of the play on Broadway: "A second visit to *Blue Denim* confirms an initial impression that, from a literary point of view, it falls a little short. It is written in the naturalistic style, which is relatively objective and inhibits the authors from making the kind of personal statement that Tennessee Williams, for example, imparts to his dramas. . . . [It] robs *Blue Denim* of some of the richness and eloquence the characters deserve. Except for the naturalistic style, it could be as poetic and memorable as *The Dark at the Top of the Stairs, The Glass Menagerie,* and *The Member of the Wedding.*"[18]

Atkinson is right to label the play naturalistic. The "through-the-keyhole" exposé enabled both Williams and Herlihy to convey the familiar world of the home and the often unpalatable social issues it hides from public view. In later works Herlihy would learn how to mix the social and temporal specifics of realism with a more penetrating understanding of the psychology of particular characters. Atkinson's judgment, that naturalism "robs *Blue Denim* of some of the richness and eloquence," is similarly astute, but the use of the term "some" is key: what is left includes symbolic material that offers an interesting commentary on, and goes below the surface of, the play's development of character and plot. A brief look at this material clarifies this point.

In *American Drama, 1940–1960: A Critical History,* Thomas Adler sees a particular strain of symbolism being employed onstage: "To some degree or other, these dramatists, perhaps reflecting the suspicions and paranoia of the McCarthy era, write about the notion of freedom in one of its many guises: the individual versus the constraints of a patriarchal society; the development of a moral relativism as an antidote to a too restrictive religious authority; and even, when focusing on the marriage relationship, the potential sacrifice of individuality and the objectification and victimization that one partner might experience at the hands of the other."[19]

Adler's suggestion certainly offers a deeper understanding of plays such as *Death of a Salesman* and *A Streetcar Named Desire* (1947). In both dramas there is a symbolism of death that can also be seen in *Blue Denim*. In the latter play the "crucifix-shaped clothes pole" in the yard, for instance, is a permanent fixture of the set that draws on Christian imagery of the New Testament (3). Like the tree in Samuel Beckett's existential drama *Waiting for Godot* (1954), which reminds us of the banality of everyday life, the pole is a semiotic of sacrifice. For some members of the audience, the sacrifice is an unborn baby. However, the symbolism is purposely vague and could also relate to the sense of loss that permeates the entire performance: Janet's loss of innocence; Jessie's lack of identity outside the roles constructed by a domestic ideology; the disappearance of childhood; and the death of individual liberty. Says Lillian, "I feel as if our whole family has just—died!" (104). As much as *Blue Denim* is about the nature of freedom in society—the freedom to be what you want, the freedom to choose—it is also about the real dangers facing young pregnant women in back-street abortion clinics.

But this is still 1958, and freedom is a lot easier to talk about than are the specific dangers of illegal abortions. Although Herlihy and Noble cannot document the specifics of the operation, they can use symbolism to engage an audience's attention on the issue. Alongside the appearance of Christian imagery, then, is the motif of bleeding. For example, Arthur's cutting himself on a broken glass prompts his mother to say, "We don't want blood poisoning" (68). This outburst echoes Ernie's anxiety about Janet's operation: "Say he uses a dirty knife or something and Janet got blood poisoning" (53). Arthur seems to recognize Janet's operation as a potential sacrifice of her life and attempts to mirror that by tearing the bandage on his hand and reopening the wound. It is this gesture, done by Arthur in a desperate attempt to feel the pain of the operation, that is denigrated by Ernie as a "big cry-baby-act" (77). As a result we feel the seriousness of the issue of abortion and its dangers being elevated to center stage.

What we have in *Blue Denim,* to borrow Christopher Bigsby's reading of Tennessee Williams, is not a hostility "to an art of surfaces," but an attempt to represent and understand the surface of familial life.[20] Herlihy and Noble achieved this by intermixing controversial issues such as abortion and lack of sexual education with a breakdown of communication in the family. As Jessie (echoing Mr. Antolini in *The Catcher in the Rye*) says, "All the children have got too big for their britches" (103). But by the end of the play, the Bartleys have gone from being a household insulated from the issues confronting American society in the 1950s to a family that has gained some knowledge of another less-visible and more-horrible world. It is not quite an awakening, but for a generation emerging out of what Robert Lowell called "the tranquilized fifties" to the eve of the 1960s, it is a start.[21]

CHAPTER 3

The Sleep of Baby Filbertson and Other Stories

In the summer of 1953 Anaïs Nin observed a particular style emerging in Herlihy's diaries, where "he transcends the direct action and produces what I call the equivalent of jazz in writing. He has rhythm and flashes of insight."[1] Nin pleaded with her friend to use that style, a quintessentially American idiom, in his fiction. *The Sleep of Baby Filbertson and Other Stories* (1959) shows that Herlihy took that advice.[2] Moving away from the realism that limited *Blue Denim,* a number of the stories in this collection are shaped by a "jazz tempo,"[3] retaining a portrait of urban lives while probing the complexities of their unconscious. Haunted by the baggage of their past, their lives move toward some form of revelation or truth about themselves. Like all of Herlihy's characters, they are fundamentally misfits, driven by a need to mask the absurdity of their lives and escape loneliness.

The title story, "The Sleep of Baby Filbertson," appeared in the *Paris Review* in 1953 and marked the beginning of Herlihy's career as a published writer.[4] The story portrays the destructive relationship between a mother, Daisy Filbertson, and her teenage son Rudy. Theirs is a relationship frustrated by an addiction to sleeping pills. Perhaps as a result or as a cause of this addiction, Daisy has a "strange restlessness" (13) that keeps them moving from city to city—San Francisco, Santa Fe, Chicago, and now New York—movement that makes their lives seem pointless. They are not the equivalent of modern pioneers, as could be said of Herlihy's other characters such as Joe Buck in *Midnight Cowboy* or Gloria Random in *The Season of the Witch,* who travel to Manhattan to carve out new lives. Rather they are fugitives from something in their past, a moment that has become repressed within their unconscious.

Like all the stories in the collection, "The Sleep of Baby Filbertson" reflects the epigraph's use of Sherwood Anderson's analogy to "gnarled, twisted apples." Both characters are obese, and their bodies are described by each other in grotesque, animalistic terms. Rudy is a "*real* hog" whose toes are "like uncooked sausages" and "breasts [are] as full as a young girl's" (11, 10). Daisy is a "nasty cartoon bulldog" or a "hibernating bear" with fat, clawlike hands (14). As in the bedroom scene that opens the narrative, Rudy is accustomed to calling his mother a "sonofabitch," and she is clearly used to slapping her son hard across the face (9). The insulting language and abusive behavior show not only a distinct lack of mutual respect and self-respect but also the same breakdown in family ties and communication that appears throughout Herlihy's writing. This tension is exacerbated by the weather, as New York "seemed to have been submerged in an ocean of hot light" (13). That atmosphere exposes characters' vulnerabilities, the "hot light" also being a nod to the naturalism of writers such as Émile Zola and Theodore Dreiser, who represented the city as a laboratory of human frailty.

On the surface Daisy's frustration seems to be fueled by two things. First, she is an agoraphobic, though one in denial about her condition. Although she makes excuses for her phobia—waiting for an imaginary telegram or backache—she never actually leaves their three-room apartment in New York. As Herlihy writes, "It was as if Daisy had reached a point in her living at which she suspected that life held no further promise, and rather than risk finding this true, she went through it grumbling, complaining, partially hypnotized by sleeping capsules, her unconscious mind artfully avoiding contact with whatever remained to be experienced" (14). Second, her frustration is fueled by Rudy. Without a job, staying in bed until the afternoon, and perpetually daydreaming, Rudy has become a symbol of his mother's insecurities, a mirror where she charts her own development or regression. But Daisy is not alone in experiencing feelings of insecurity. Even though Rudy spends each day wandering around the city, his time is spent attempting to escape reality. The movies offer this sense of escape, but his dream of being their romantic hero is haunted by the realization that his only hope of working in Hollywood is "in funny fat-person parts" (10).

The story centers on a particular day when Rudy travels into the city to see a movie starring Ginger Rogers. While he is on the subway, the narrative recounts his memory of an incident in which he was driving in Louisiana when he became transfixed by a young black man leaning against a lamppost. As a result of taking his eyes off the road, Rudy crashed the car through the window of a furniture store, knocking a policeman onto one of the display beds. A number of features of this memory stand out. The first is that Rudy emerges from the memory overwhelmed by hysterical laughter, as he did in the actual incident. As David Gillady experiences in "Laughter in the Graveyard," also in *The Sleep of Baby Filbertson,* such hysteria is a result of the repression of trauma. But the repressed never remains hidden in Herlihy's writing. Rather it haunts his characters; it pursues them wherever they go. Unraveling that trauma offers an important means of understanding "The Sleep of Baby Filbertson."

It is interesting that the dream is set in Louisiana, as the context represents the last "settled" home. But that home also represents "nothing but trouble" (12). It is difficult for the reader to understand the exact nature of that trouble, but it seems likely that it involved Daisy's husband, Rudy's father, who was (deservedly it seems) committed to a psychiatric hospital. Carl Jung's saying "To proceed from the dream outward," used by Nin throughout her work, is particularly useful here.[5] Dreams, after all, help the reader connect one narrative image with another. Since the accident, the young black man has become almost a permanent figure in Rudy's imagination. What is particularly striking about this figure, or at least Rudy's memory of him, is a scar shaped like a sickle, "which stretched from his left ear to his Adam's apple and then descended down the length of his throat" (13). The question is whether the man's scar, the car accident, and the transience and addiction of a mother and son have any association with their home life in Louisiana and the father's committal. Is that the trauma that Daisy and Rudy are attempting to escape?

These questions are never answered, of course, but they are hinted at in the following scene. As Rudy comes out of the cinema and crosses the road, he is engrossed in opening a packet of caramel corn rather than aware of the oncoming traffic. As a result he is hit by an oncoming car: "Rudy's right hand was bruised where he tried to break his fall, and in his left, as if it had been the widow's baby snatched in the nick of time from the burning house, he clutched the white sack of caramel corn" (16). The simile is intriguing, coming at a time when an accident promotes a rapid memory of the past as it begins to expose detail of another context. Here close reading reveals the specific nature of the subject: not just any old widow but "the widow"; not just any old burning house but "the burning house." The terms help readers understand that there is a familiar relationship between Rudy and this other context. But this leads only to further questions: What house was burning? Was it a house in Louisiana? Was it connected with the young black man or, indeed, Rudy's father? Is this the "trouble" in the past hinted at in the narrative?

Rather than answer those questions directly, the narrative establishes a parallel between the past—in fact a dream of the past—and the events surrounding the accident in the present. As Rudy gets up off the sidewalk and walks away with only minor injuries, he is followed by a young black man who urges him to get a taxi home. The man has what seems to be the same sicklelike scar on his neck as the figure in the dream, and his presence makes Rudy feel "stark naked," a conventional literary metaphor of truth being exposed (16). The stranger's name is Clyde Williams, and as in the dream, he waves goodbye to Rudy while leaning on a lamppost. After Rudy returns home, Daisy is typically unsympathetic and irritable. As she sadistically tends his wound with iodine, their conversation reveals overt racism. For Rudy, Clyde is "some coon" and "a black idiot" (19, 21); Daisy is outraged that he "let a nigger shove you on the sidewalk" (19). Despite brushing off the racism, Rudy goes to bed convinced that Clyde is the young black man from Louisiana who has followed him to New York. That anxiety of being pursued leads to the second key dream of the story.

In that dream Rudy is taken by a band of black gypsies into a lonely forest in the Deep South. When Rudy is tied to a tree alongside a raging fire, a female gypsy severs his genitals from his body with a knife. It is difficult to ignore the associations with lynching in this dream. As an extreme articulation of southern racism was still prevalent during the 1950s, the Filbertsons would have been aware of lynching. Yet Rudy's dream represents a reversal of that form of racial lynching. Perhaps by placing himself as its victim there is guilt, which exposes an unconscious wish to be punished or at least take the place of somebody who has been punished. If this reading were pushed, then Daisy, her husband, and Rudy could be considered as being somehow involved in the lynching of Clyde Williams, who wears the scar of such an assault on his neck. As in Toni Morrison's *Beloved,* Clyde can be understood as a ghost, a manifestation of the guilt hidden in a family's unconscious. To believe in this guilt also offers some understanding as to why Daisy and Rudy spend their lives seemingly running away from something.

Rudy is awakened from this dream by Clyde's tapping at the window. As Rudy looks outside, though, Clyde has vanished, and all there is for Rudy to gaze at is an old elm tree. An interesting choice of Herlihy's, the elm, like the poplar in Billie Holiday's song "Strange Fruit" (1939), was used to hang black bodies in the American South and for switches for beatings. The dream and the following hallucination create a fear so overwhelming that they lead Rudy in a desperate search for his mother's sleeping pills. Believing, wrongly, that Daisy is asleep, he steals a pill from her night table. This inevitably leaves the reader with the following, perhaps unanswerable, question: in feigning sleep, why does Daisy ensure that "her nightgown was torn and one of her breasts was revealed" (23)? Indeed, Daisy's demand to "Come kiss your mother, goddamit!" now seems disturbing, made worse by Rudy's response that she could "go to hell" (24). Although nothing more is made of the nuances of this moment, overbearing—bordering on incestuous—relationships between mothers and children recur in *All Fall Down* (1960). The sleeping pill, though, serves only as a temporary respite and is no cure for their condition. In offering his readers no closure, Herlihy's first published story is one of the most unsettling of his career.

By far the longest story in the collection, "The Summer of the Dead" is set in the San Gabriel Valley in California at the start of the 1950s.[6] This is another story in which "heat, smog and humidity made a hell" (26). Here, Wesley Stuart lives in the top-floor apartment of a rooming house in Pasadena. Wesley's life is shaped by a routine that is as stifling as the summer heat. Each day he drives to and from Hollywood, where he works as a carpenter building sets for a television station. He prefers his own company, acquaintances to friends, and saving to spending. As in "The Sleep of Baby Filbertson," this story is not about literal death but rather a symbolic death-in-life.

The reasons for Wesley's self-imposed isolation from the world are rooted in his past. Unlike the previous story, the details of this past are made explicit. In a small city in central Ohio, he was brought up by a family at war with themselves. The constant arguments, his father's drinking and overbearing attitude, his mother's "agony of unfulfilment, bitterness" all resulted in withdrawal from a social world. But as is often the case in Herlihy's writing, the baggage of the past remains with the character, and so Wesley would sometimes experience "sudden flashes of clarity in which he could see in himself his father's image" (36). His escape is as much from that image of his father within as it is from the past: "From any relationship not directly involved with earning his livelihood, he automatically withdrew. And he nurtured this isolation with the loving care of a mother for a child for within it he was at peace" (37).

The point of the story, then, is to shatter that peace. All of the characters who live in the rooming house can be understood as vehicles for unsettling Wesley's day-to-day routine and exposing him to the truth of an emotionally repressed self. This process begins with the landlady, Mrs. Kromer, who is convinced that Wesley's silent attitude, his reluctance to socialize, is caused by a "troubled soul" (42). With nothing to do all day except drink lemon juice on the front porch and meditate on her favorite books by Anna Hope Barneweller, Mrs. Kromer believes that companionship is a cure for this trouble.

The other resident who plays a role in trying to cure Wesley is Faye Selger. Faye had married young and moved out west, but her husband died in World War II. No longer a teenager, she traveled to Hollywood to make a life in the movies. While waiting for an opportunity to come along, her days are filled with working at a cosmetics counter and her evenings gossiping and drinking lemon juice with Mrs. Kromer on the front porch. It is clear for all, including Mrs. Kromer, that Faye has eyes for Wesley, and her flirting is an attempt to make him notice her.

Both Mrs. Kromer and Faye are desperately lonely characters. Like Wesley, Faye is haunted by the events in her life: "When pressed further on this subject or on any other for which the truth was inconvenient she would turn her face squarely to the person sitting next to her . . . and smile, knitting her brows in a way that suggested some mysterious never-to-be-forgotten pain: 'Lover,' she would say, 'if there is one subject that absolutely and surely depresses me, it is the past'" (40). Mrs. Kromer is also haunted by the past, or at least a dream of a past that has lodged itself in her imagination. Indeed she admits to Wesley that "you and me just might—just *might,* I say, be bearing the same cross" (46). This "cross" alludes to a lost love, a Chinaman, whom she sees often in meditations and dreams but has never once met in person. Mrs. Kromer imagines every aspect of this man's life—his wife, his children, his unhappiness—and realizes that his sadness comes from their not having met and thus fulfilling their destiny.

The separate rooms of the house function as a metaphor for separate, unfulfilled lives. They are lonesome, a term preached by Mr. O'Daniel in *Midnight Cowboy* and a key word underpinning Herlihy's major recurring themes. Faye's room, for instance, is "dark and untidy" and represents the incompleteness of her past experience and present life (38). She spends as little time as she can in this room, preferring to sit outside in the hall or on the porch waiting for the opportunity to flirt with Wesley. In contrast, Wesley has built himself a self-constructed prison that represents a flight from reality. Here he is able to walk around naked, take baths, and enjoy the silence of his own company without having intrusion from any other person.

This solitude ends with the introduction into the narrative of Earl Walker, a blind and deaf salesman who moves into the room next to Wesley's. His direct interruption of Wesley's life, as he walks into Wesley's room while Wesley is naked, is not accidental. Although Earl turns up looking for a room while he is virtually penniless, Mrs. Kromer, for whom nothing is coincidental, believes that Earl "had been sent to teach Wesley Stuart a lesson" (71). Her plan to end Wesley's isolation could not have worked out better. The characters become firm friends, and Earl comes to Wesley for his meals. After all, Earl is the perfect friend for Wesley. He hardly speaks and, being unable to see and hear, ensures Wesley's obsession with privacy. As the companionship interrupts the loneliness of Herlihy's characters, it also imbues Wesley with a renewed energy. Driving home from work, for instance, "he drove faster across the speedway, ran more quickly than ever up the stairs to the forth floor and prepared elaborate substantial meals in place of the quick carry-out salads and cold cuts from the delicatessen which had previously satisfied him" (55).

Earl's presence, indeed his blindness and deafness, helps readers understand the nuances Herlihy has invested in characterization. All characters exist in some sort of blindness, their dimly lit rooms and unfulfilled routines sheltering them from having to engage with the reality of life. But Wesley's character can be seen as hiding a more significant nuance. According to Herlihy, there are three homosexual characters, whom he does not name, in *The Sleep of Baby Filbertson.*[7] "The Summer of the Dead" offers readers certain clues that may point to Wesley's repressed homosexuality. When he was a child, his drunken father instilled in him "ways in which a 'man' does not behave" (35). The caution marks around "man" are telling, as they reveal that Wesley's gender, his sexuality, has been constructed on the surface and repressed in the unconscious. As ever in Herlihy's work, the truth emerges in dreams. A recurring dream for Wesley has him wandering into a morgue where he sees a corpse. He always wakes from this dream in hysterical tears, leaving Mrs. Kromer, who listened in one evening, to conclude that the corpse was Wesley. The reasons behind this dream are clear for Mrs. Kromer: Wesley is a bachelor whose soul has died because he has given up the need for love.

Faye certainly tries to fill that void in Wesley's life. She flirts with him in his room by taking off her dress supposedly because of the heat and by caressing his hair, face, and hands. But Wesley is not moved by these advances, and in his rejection of them Faye has a moment of insight into Wesley's isolation that helps her allude to his sexuality. As they both explain to Mrs. Kromer why Faye was in Wesley's room without a dress on, the following conversation occurs:

> "Don't worry about it, Mrs. Kromer. Faye's safe with me."
>
> Faye looked into his face for a moment, her eyes opened wide, and she said loudly: "Safe! Did you say *safe*?" And then she began to laugh. Wesley felt the blood rush to his face again as her laughter rose. Faye threw herself into the chair next to Mrs. Kromer. She turned to her and said, "Honey, did you hear what I heard?"
>
> Mrs. Kromer was puzzled. "I think I did. Why?"
>
> "Oh, nothing, but it just struck me. Sit down, Wes."

> But Wesley remained standing, his toes gripped firmly at the soles of his shoes as if he sought to plant himself more securely to the wooden planks of the porch floor. He looked at Faye and he saw her eyes glittering wildly into his face and now Mrs. Kromer was staring at him too.
>
> "A girl couldn't be *safer,*" Faye said. "She just couldn't!" (62)

Everything about this short exchange suggests a revelation by the women and Wesley's annoyance at having been found out. The eyes of both female characters penetrate into a truth that for so long has been hidden. The fact that "safer" is in italics highlights the force of this revelation for Faye. Wesley's physical mannerism is defensive, suggesting that something intimate has been revealed. This is a key moment, and its place in the narrative is crucial, as it helps the reader understand another important scene that follows.

The friendship with Earl does go through a rough patch, and Wesley seeks his own solitude once again. But Wesley cannot return to this solitude in the same way, and as the season changes from summer to the mildness of early fall, the reader sees evidence of a distinct closeness developing in their relationship. This closeness prompts Earl to read Wesley's face by using his hands. The result is one of the most erotic moments in the collection:

> For a brief moment this smooth open palm rested against his cheek and then suddenly the fingers, infinitely gentle, began quickly to explore his face, stopping now and again as if to memorize what they had found. Wesley thought he had never experienced such profound tenderness, and because he was trembling, he gripped the table firmly to prevent Earl from detecting his emotion. Wesley had learned to find in the movement of Earl's hands all that might be found in the eyes of a person with sight; and now when Earl's hand hesitated for a moment he knew that during this pause some knowledge was being registered in the blind man's brain . . . Earl removed the napkin from his lap, rose from the table, excused himself and left the room. Wesley walked over to the door and closed it. Then he lay down on the bed and dropped a soft white pillow on to his face. (80–81)

Apart from this being a startlingly beautiful and moving passage, it may offer some circumstantial evidence of Wesley's homosexuality through his growing love for his friend. As such, the "reading" is transformed into a caress and is meant to parallel Faye's sexualized touching of Wesley's face, lips, and hands, which he rejected much earlier in the story.

The fact that Earl found some secret knowledge in reading Wesley's face, which compelled him to leave the room, does not at first seem to alter their friendship. They still take long drives to the mountains and the beach. But there is a hint that something is not quite right with the relationship. Earl, for instance, now makes himself scarce during the week, and Wesley sees him only at mealtimes. Wesley's dream may hold a premonition of their impending separation. The dream involves Wesley and Earl, now not blind, building an airplane. Their flight takes them above the houses and then crashes into Mrs. Kromer's lawn. Earl walks away from the crash unscathed, but Wesley is dead, that is until Mrs. Kromer performs a miracle by summoning him back to life.

Like most dreams in literature, this one is complex and codified. In one sense it feels similar to the dream of flight that Shirley experiences with her dead brother in *All Fall Down*. That dream is about reconnecting with something lost. Wesley's dream seems similar; rising above the world is, then, a symbolic act that parallels a rising out of the character's unconscious to connect with true feelings. What started with the summer of the dead can now end with rebirth. But Earl does walk away from Wesley's body, which establishes a new separation between the two characters. This separation is fundamental to what actually happens immediately after the dream. When Wesley knocks on Earl's door to remind him that it is the start of their weekend, a semiclothed Faye answers. As she talks of her growing relationship with Earl, Wesley's violent response resembles the jealousy and rage of a jilted and gay lover. Shocked by the violence, Mrs. Kromer collapses and dies; her death reflects the literalness of the story's title. Ultimately, though, Wesley's return to his room before locking the door symbolizes the continuation of death-in-life and a metaphor of a summer of love turned sour.

In contrast to Wesley's repression, Lizzie Ballinet in "Jazz of Angels" "wears on the outside what most people wear on the inside" (87). Set in Hollywood, the story charts a day in the life of Lizzie. Wandering the streets, talking to herself, reliving a moment in the past, Lizzie is a common spectacle of urban alienation. Belonging more to the past, she represents a misfit in the present, and this is what shifts the narrative from a realistic concern with lost lives to a surrealism of unconscious visions. All of Herlihy's characters seem stuck in a past moment from which they are trying to escape. Lizzie's "moment" was during the 1930s, when she worked as a minor actress in crowd scenes and a reader of tea leaves for the stars. But it is the death of a friend, called Miss D. on a movie set, that is the central trauma of her life and the moment in which she is stuck. Although the closure of the studio, which seems to end her film career, is significant, it is clearly subordinate to the death of Miss D.

The realism begins with a ritual: Lizzie "reports . . . each day as a matter of discipline" to the locked gates of the studio (87). The ritual is telling and exposes the emptiness of her life. But words such as "reports" and "discipline" also point to the ritual as a form of self-punishment. It is difficult to know whether this punishment is a result of the death of Miss D. After all, the narrative does not offer detail except for Lizzie's often-incoherent mumbling to herself and others on Hollywood Boulevard. Those "mumblings" are important, though, as they show that Lizzie carries around guilt for Miss D.'s lonely life and death. She wears that guilt in the lines that tell stories on her face, a guilt that serves to fragment her perception of the world around her.

Ian Hugo's loosely based adaptation of "Jazz of Angels" into the short sixteen-minute experimental film *Jazz of Lights* (1954) plays on that fragmentation. The film, set in New York's Times Square, has no obvious characters. Rather it is a film preoccupied with what Nin calls "an ephemeral flow of sensations" endemic to urban life.[8] In the original story, these sensations result in the juxtaposition and fluidity of past and present. The ephemeral nature of these sensations is reflected in jazz, that quintessentially urban art form that had represented discord when used in the cinema of Elia Kazan and Otto Preminger. Herlihy uses jazz to probe the complexity of characters, their secret recesses of wish and will, what Nin might label "cities of the interior."[9]

Herlihy structures a narrative that operates by continually moving between internal and external perspectives, and this operation is stimulated by jazz: "When the music of a jazz band emanating from a cocktail bar along the boulevard reaches her ears it somehow keeps going inside of her, fills her body and excludes everything else. Three or four bars of this blue rhythm are enough to transform the street into a garden party. Lizzie begins to dance and there are people who stop and watch, some laughing, pointing her out, others jeering and applauding; and there are even a few who stand with quiet reverence in the face of the projection of a secret life of another. There are remarks and automobile horns and police whistles—but these noises find no mark in Lizzie's mind; they mingle with the jazz and soon the medley comes to an end with one strong ensemble break" (88–89). "Projection" is the key term of this passage, offering readers a visualization of the secret "life of another." But the projector does not maintain continuity, and the result is akin to the stream of consciousness that underpins jazz, the randomness that produces flashes of insight that quickly flitter out and die.

Arriving in Hollywood from Nebraska in the 1920s, Lizzie would have been engulfed by the remnants of the Jazz Age. Compared with the domestic conformity of the 1950s, the flapper culture celebrated increased sexual freedom for women. Like Blanche DuBois in Tennessee Williams's *A Streetcar*

Named Desire (1947), Lizzie lives mentally in that prewar world, where she is young, pretty, and knowingly attractive to men. As such she retains that same adolescent flirtation in the present: "'Don't frown, young man, you'll wrinkle yourself early!' She sends a kiss traveling on the air towards him, and turns away, chastising herself gently" (90). As Blanche uses bromide and whiskey to numb her experience in a new and alienating American South, so Lizzie sees her world through a film of tears, which muffle her senses. As is the case for Wesley Stuart and Daisy Filbertson, complete withdrawal for Lizzie signals a symbolic form of death. In Herlihy's world only the characters who can find the strength to push beyond that can survive.

After walking all day, Lizzie returns to an empty home, though she continues to hear chimes in her head. For characters who live alone in empty houses, TV has a particular function to help fill the void of emptiness, silence, and darkness. Lizzie immediately switches on the TV and replies to the man's voice selling orange juice. What happens next is interesting because it echoes Wesley's habit when he returns to his room in the heat: "There is a series of removals: a hat, a wig, a coat, a dress, a petticoat, a pair of panties, a brassiere, a pair of stockings" (92). The symbolism here is certainly psychological as much as it is physical, making public the secrets of the character's heart and mind.

The appearance of six angels marks the end of Lizzie's story, as the tolling of the Angelus Bell marks its beginning. The angels are from the Swan Lake Casino and are a dreamlike extension of the TV show to which Lizzie falls asleep. Angels are messengers, delivering pieces of urgent information. The urgency involves how one should deal with a stranger on the street. The narrative's conclusion is to "surround her as softly as light falling on a new earth" and "love you I love you I love you" (94). It is the sadness of lost connections in an imperfect world, but the loss is ours: the spectators' and not the subject's. "Love Letter to a Mad Woman" is one of the original titles Herlihy thought about using for this story, a title that implicitly calls for attention to be paid to such a person as Lizzie.[10]

Like Daisy Filbertson and Mrs. Kromer, the central character of "Pretty on the Bus at Night Time" is obese. It is another story of the collection to be written in the first-person voice of the character, a style that Herlihy would develop in *The Season of the Witch,* and it represents a confessional of the self-inflicted guilt and loneliness of being different. Irene feels guilty on two counts. The first relates to her husband, Hugo, leaving home three years previously. Her life has seemingly stuck in that moment. The second relates to her young daughter, Melody, who is without a father. The guilt is wrapped up with her obesity, which she sees as a disease. The cure is simple: to search for and find a husband. It is that condition, and an inability to find a cure, that represents a metaphor for the whole story, making her as lonesome as the rest of Herlihy's characters.

That "sickness" is difficult to treat. Even a letter to a lonely-hearts column is seen as "a shot of penicillin in the ocean to cure it from being deep" (96). Without the cure, Irene spends her nights cleaning doctors' offices and her days looking after her daughter and lodging house. It is here, while washing clothes one day, that her hand and hair slip into the wringer, making her feel "worse than a sick horse." The lack of concentration, which caused the accident, may have been caused by "shots which are supposed to make you slim" but which seem to inhibit sleep and cause irritability (97). The accident shows her that she must do something drastic with her life in order to get a husband. With that comes a perfect life; without that, life is lonesomeness and obesity.

To fulfill her dream Irene does what a number of Herlihy's characters do: that is, board a bus and ride to a new town where there is at least hope of a new life. As such, she takes up a job in an army camp, keeping shop in a military hospital. The fact that her work always seems to be associated with medical institutions effectively affirms the nature of her quest. In the hospital she meets Sergeant R. D. Burklemaster, who was originally from the mountains of North Carolina. After a brief courtship consisting of trips to the cinema and a bar, and one sexual act that she sees as a sin, they agree to get married. The attraction to him, though, is not just because he would make a good father to Melody but also because he treats Irene like "a puppy not weighing in at no two hundred and sixty pounds." To be light, in Irene's book, is to be young: "It was like he was Hugo and I was a young girl. When he looked at me I felt as pretty and skinny as a statue standing in the middle of a fountain in the park somewhere" (105, 106).

Burklemaster is a character who exploits the vulnerable. He seems as much obsessed with money and drink as Irene is by her weight. Having taken Irene's eighty-four dollars and last being seen boarding a plane back to North Carolina, he does not show up for the wedding. His absence only serves to confirm her low self-esteem, and with this feeling she boards the bus to return home. It is here, for the second time, that Melody utters the title of the story. On both occasions, the first being the journey to the army camp, Melody says, "It's pretty on the bus at night-time." The difference in Irene's reaction is startling. During the trip to the camp, the phrase reminds Irene that children have an eye for beauty and an ability to dream. But on return, Irene slaps her daughter hard across the face: "It is a job to teach them, to give them the right kind of heart, to dry them up young" (112). In showing how a parent's poor life experience is passed on to their children, Herlihy establishes what will become a major theme in his fiction.

If there are three homosexual characters in "The Sleep of Baby Filbertson," "Miguel" must include the second. An attractive eighteen-year-old man, Miguel has traveled from his native Uruguay and his beloved Mamacita to New Orleans and then, in the company of a salesman called Eric, onto San Francisco. Stealing money from Eric exposes an initial flaw in Miguel's character. Despite being racked with a short-lived guilt, Miguel's unconscious search for love, which would bring a sense of belonging to a place, is tempered by his inability or unwillingness to make the leap into the unknown. The peculiar romance of the city's cable cars, their intersecting paths allowing the passengers to gaze at each other for a fleeting moment, is used as a metaphor for just that: "Now there is that briefest of all moments when the two cable cars pass midway up the hill, and stop only a few inches apart. *Her* desire, pure as a white angel towering over a Christmas tree, reaches into the space between you where your eyes meet. Unpleading, uncompromising, there is a moment of interlocking thought: I could love such a one as you, as you, love you I love you, and the impulse to leap on to the descending car is strongest now . . . but one does not leap. . . . What is wrong with a world in which one does not leap across the infinitesimal gap of time and space which separates him from his love?" (115; emphasis added). The reader is meant to substitute the word "his" for "her." In a story that crosses into the secret world of gay lives during the 1950s, such references are necessarily coded. Although Herlihy has come closer than any other writer of the period in broaching that world, there still exists the "infinitesimal gap" between longing and public utterance that he dare not cross by employing realistic detail.

Like other stories in this volume, "Miguel" is based on a sense of separation from an engagement with everyday life. As such, the narrative takes its readers into that separate life. Edward, a young man whom Miguel meets while wandering around the streets, represents a guide into "a secret place": "There was a sign on the door which said: For Members Only. Up two flights of stairs, through a corridor and beyond an archway, there was a large barroom filled with men of all types and sizes" (116). Miguel's beauty makes him a star attraction to the men in this club, but their desperation only exposes their own loneliness. Of course, being the 1950s, there are no details of the sexual act between Miguel and Edward. All the reader knows is that they went to bed together and that Edward leaves him the taxi fare to return to his hotel room.

The crux of all these stories, though, is to expose the truth of characters to themselves. The character who serves to establish this exposé is Carl, who lives on and maintains a boat in Marin County. Moving in with Carl, Miguel experiences "an invitation to breathe" (118), which is one of a series of symbolisms that point the way to a sense of liberation, the ability to create oneself anew: "Miguel worked hard on the boat, alone much of the time, while Carl applied color to the large door-size canvas for which his Latin friend had posed. Miguel was sorry he had taken money from some of the Americans without having earned it; he scraped and chipped away the old dead paint until the boards were bare" (119). Stripping the wood of the boat in preparation for new paint clearly symbolizes the changes awaiting Miguel. As Wesley is changed by caring for his friend Earl in "The Summer of the Dead," Miguel is slowly transformed by caring for someone other than himself. The narrative allows readers to understand the significance of this change by comparing Miguel to Christ. The pair of eyes, which are painted on the front of the boat signaling its completion, "was Christ, his Resurrection, a pure white Jesus, ascending into Heaven, and the face of Christ was Miguel's" (120).

If this is love, as Miguel's letter to his mother might suggest, then it is short-lived. As soon as the painting on the boat is completed, either Miguel seems to want to move on or Carl wants to be on his own. Thus the wine and food both characters partake of represent a Last Supper. As Miguel's letter to his mother says, he has won and now lost "a girl." The fact that "the girl" is dead shows the finality of their relationship (121). The enveloping fog heightens that sense of separation and isolation of characters. The end of the story takes us back to its beginning, and we realize that Miguel is moving from city to city, from room to room, clearly trapped in this lonely life. Miguel, frustrated and fixated on his mother, is unable to love as a gay man and can seek sexual encounters only at night or locked away in boats. He had the opportunity for companionship. In *Midnight Cowboy,* Joe Buck takes that opportunity. The flaw in Miguel, as with most of the characters in this collection, is that he cannot.

"Laughter in the Graveyard" is the only other first-person narrative in the collection. As with Irene in "Pretty on the Bus at Nighttime," fourteen-year-old David Gillady reflects on a particular moment in his life. From the beginning of the story, his perspective is on seventeen-year-old Steve Kurkowski, who lives with his Polish parents in the house opposite David's. The houses are typical of postwar suburbia as pictured in *Blue Denim.* It is this background that elevates Steve to the status of "somebody special" (123).

Steve has a heart condition and is slowly dying, a fact that makes him experience a profound sense of loneliness. With some conspiring by his sister,

Delores, and David's mother, the two teenagers are brought together. So develops a close friendship that is based on literal and symbolic forms of death. For David, Steve is a prince who lives not in a house like his own but in a palace with turrets on the roof. The reasons for this coloring of characterization are complex. He looks at Steve wanting in effect to be him. It is Steve's ability to deal with death while appearing strong, independent, and aloof that impresses most of all: "I saw something new in Steve's eyes, a quality of inhumanly perfect remoteness." We learn also that Steve keeps "a fascinating memoir composed of dreams and truth" and also teaches David the spiritual qualities of jazz (127, 128). What are means for dealing with his condition become David's first inspiration, a signal of the symbolic death of his own childhood and the birth of a more mature self that is able to deal with personal trauma.

That trauma relates to his father, Edwin, who is "a strange man." Prone to bouts of violent temper and alcoholism, Edwin practices a routine of abuse on his son in order to "knock out princely ways," while his mother worries only about the neighbors (129). Edwin senses that his son's "princely ways" results from a different kind of masculinity than the one proscribed by the hegemony of postwar gender stereotypes. To escape his father's clutches, David alters his daily routine. As the following beautifully written prose indicates, he begins to carve out a private an ultimate space of his own:

> Instead of going straight home that evening, I walked several blocks to the public school on Euclid Avenue where there was a lawn, the biggest patch of grass you could find in our area of Cleveland. The snow was melted and the earth was dry enough that you could do some lying down and looking up at the sky, a fine pastime in any decent weather, and that's what I did for maybe an hour or two while hundreds of horn-honking cars rolled by on the streets like noisy lightning bugs; two cats fought as they made love in the bushes under a schoolroom window; early spring insects buzzed a street lamp like crazy Indians dancing for rain. It was hard to imagine there being no more living on this earth, until some black heavy clouds moved in from nowhere, soggy-looking clouds that got in the way of the stars. (129)

The black clouds signal Steve's death. However, the fact that it is springtime also points to the traditional cliché of the rebirth toward which David is heading. The seeds of this mature self allow David, in reflection of the past, to forgive his father.

Even with the memory of parental violence, the narrative focuses on two events that are highly symbolic. The first happens during Steve's funeral service, after David and his father have remained with the body all night to honor Mr. Kurkowski's Polish tradition. Unable to cry during the service, David begins to laugh uncontrollably. Even his mother recognizes this as a form of hysteria. But it is also a sign of an emotion having been repressed, unable to articulate itself in an equally repressed ideology that his parents represent. The second event comes from David's memory of his father's falling into the open grave. The moment occurs in what he calls "jazz time, in which the sins of all the people concerned, even my father's, seemed to have been forgiven." His father's symbolic burial results in much laughter, rendering him and his situation absurd. The "new grass," a baptism of rain that "made the earth lovely," and "the soft white light of clouds" that accompanies the detail of the scene also show David's rebirth into a mature, liberated, and forgiving protagonist (140). As in all of Herlihy's works, the past needs to be shelved, even temporarily, for the possibility of a new future.

Like Wesley Stuart, Polly Heidt in "Weeping in the Chinese Window" has built up a routine of everyday experiences that serve to shelter her from any emotional and sexual engagement with life. To achieve that, twenty-five-year-old Polly lives her life for others. By day she works as a bookkeeper for a real-estate broker. The rest of the time is devoted to her elderly father, a blind old lady called Mrs. Godspell, and the local Baptist church. She performs these duties perfectly but, like Norah in Henrik Ibsen's *A Doll's House* (1879), does retain a space for secrets. The bottle of blackberry brandy in the dresser drawer, an occasional cigarette, and a visit to the movies—a sin in the eyes of her Baptist minister—represent the possibility of liberation from constraint, as the macaroons signal the onset of Norah's rebellion from her domestic life. The tension between a surface world and an interior world is often present in Herlihy's characters. How successful they become depends on how well they listen to, and act on, a genuine desire.

Each day, walking from church, Polly would stop and gaze into the window of her favorite shop, Hi Sing's Oriental Imports. The window was always full of teas, exotic jewelry, fragrances, and elaborately decorated fans and parasols, and Polly would finger "with her eyes each pagan object." The juxtaposition of pagan and Christian worlds reflects a tension within her, a tension that creeps out through the "delicate mechanism" of weeping. This conflict is embodied in the life-size statue of the Buddha that appears one day in the window. On the surface Polly is captivated by the statue's symbolic representation of "freedom from desire." However, as the reader comes to realize and Polly is not fully aware of, she "covetously" worships the Buddha's freedom and his teaching to be oneself (144). The window, then, projects

Polly's ugliness, as she sees it, but also her need to be beautiful. In the silence that accompanies her gaze, the reader feels her need to become sexually attractive.

As if seeing the Buddha is an indication of impending change, Polly meets Howard. The chance meeting in front of the shop window is, as Herlihy knew, integral to the phantasmagorical nature of urban life. He has established this atmosphere, the same atmosphere found in Charles Baudelaire's poetic descriptions of the nineteenth-century Parisian crowd, from the beginning: "We who dwell in cities are apt to see a hundred faces or more each day, for the streetcars, drugstores, offices and elevators are filled with them. Ninety-nine times out of a hundred, the image will sift through and disappear without having made a difference in our living and doing; but when the image of a particular face lodges itself in the heart, we who dwell in cities are in for change and this is the miracle we live for" (141). Howard is one of these faces that lodges in the heart because he has bothered to breach the divide between personal and public worlds. Here, Polly feels that her dress has turned into gossamer (an interesting and antiquated word that conjures up a sense of gothic romanticism) before she becomes completely naked, that is, without the everyday garments of routine and order.

Howard is an eccentric figure, a roller coaster of different emotions that at times resembles the chaos of Dean Moriarty in Jack Kerouac's *On the Road* (1957). Like Moriarty, Howard loves driving fast and being naked in powerful cars, gazing and laughing at the ocean, and talking continuously about seemingly random subjects. He is the American anarchic voice personified in Herlihy's work, almost like the chaotic natural self deeply repressed and trapped within Polly. He is obsessed by music, and the only idiom that can perfectly reflect his being is jazz. As Nin pleaded with Herlihy to write with a quintessentially American tempo, so Howard captures that spirit in talking about the human voice: "You can scream with it, you can grunt. I mean you can moan with it, you can whimper. One instrument. And you can sing. God, it's fabulous when you think about it, not to mention just laughing. Or talking" (148).

But for all his bravado, Howard, like Polly, has a repressed interior. He has come out of World War II with a "Total Disability" that has left him a "psychoneurotic" (151). Howard sees jazz as Polly sees the Buddha, then, as a healing force, which has the power to take "single people who are lonely . . . split up in a million pieces" and "puts them together" (145–46). For a brief moment this is what happens. Their relationship develops enough for them both to go to the beach, drive into the mountains, and have sex. But Polly's inhibitions, her belief that her meeting Howard represented "the fall" and that sex is sin, hinder their relationship from developing any further (153). As a result Howard disappears, and she is left to pick up the fragments of her life, but this time numbed by brandy and interrupted by thoughts of suicide. Herlihy has taken a person from the crowd, alienated from a world of emotions, and showed her what she could have if she allowed it. But Polly cannot make the leap and so becomes, like characters in later works, just another anonymous face among millions.

CHAPTER 4

All Fall Down

Like *Blue Denim, All Fall Down* (1960) shows James Leo Herlihy's fascination with the decay of a suburban family.[1] Set in Cleveland, Ohio, during the 1950s, the novel follows the lives of the Williamses over the course of two years. They are a typical middle-class family who, like the Bartleys, move toward a central crisis. Perhaps because of Anaïs Nin's suggestion to "get deeper"[2] into the experience of his characters and the nuances of settings, Herlihy merges realism with a gothic understanding of that world. As in the work of Carson McCullers, Tennessee Williams, and Sherwood Anderson, whose representations of place and time are often shaped by protagonists' grotesque visions and emotional insecurities, *All Fall Down* is populated by neurotic parents and hard-to-reach sons who, in the midst of material comfort, live lives of quiet desperation. "It is a far less objective process than you know," Herlihy wrote to Nin in the winter of 1959, "and the novel, for instance, was deeply personal, in that the dilemma and the characters are in my own family."[3]

Since moving from their old home on Amelia Street, the Williams family members have been the subject of gossip among the inhabitants of Seminary Street. The gossip has included stories about the oldest son of the family, Berry-Berry, who went missing during the move and has never slept in his new bed. The rumors, which talk of Berry-Berry being a wild character making trouble in southern towns such as Covington, Kentucky, and Biloxi, Mississippi, are, as the reader learns, accurate. So too are the stories of his returning home at odd times in the night, parking his blue Ford pickup truck on the drive behind a Dodge touring car with a "Foreign Consul sticker on the windshield," and peeing out of an upstairs bedroom window. His absence and his eventual presence are fundamental parts of the novel's structure and characterization. However, "there was often a wide and ridiculous difference between what took place in the Williams's house and what the people of Seminary Street actually believed" (13). Although the stories reflect on the peculiarities of each character, they fail to appreciate that an emptiness left by a missing son affects each member of the family in profound ways.

The father, Ralph, is seen by the children of the neighborhood to spend large amounts of time in the basement of the house. At night especially he becomes a "grinning old man" who, laboring under lamplight, produces subversive material intent on undermining the American Way of politics and religion (11). There is some truth to this. Ralph, sixty-one and a retired real-estate dealer, has communist sympathies that date back to his hobo days in the 1930s. But what the children do not see is that, instead of writing pamphlets or receiving messages from un-American organizations, Ralph is passing time drinking Old Grandad bourbon and completing a jigsaw puzzle that he has been making and unmaking for years. He is convinced that he has let himself "get soft." Like Major Bartley in *Blue Denim,* he feels like "a peg that doesn't fit anywhere," especially upstairs in the family home where his wife, Annabel, maintains at least a semblance of domestic order (27).

Like the Major and Ralph, Jessie and Annabel have a lot in common. They are both married to men who are significantly older than them. They also conform to the archetype of the suburban housewife whose routine, pictured in the glossy magazines of the day, revolved around bringing up children, shopping, looking after their husbands, and keeping the home clean with Mr. Sheen. In addition, perhaps because of that role, both take prescription medicine to calm their feelings of frustration and anxiety. Unlike Jessie, though, who is very much part of the lady's social scene in Detroit, Annabel is viewed with a certain curiosity by the neighborhood. It is not that she is subversive like her husband or wild like her son. Instead any reputation she has comes from her behavior on the day the Williamses moved to Seminary Street. On that day she handed out marshmallows to the children who had gathered around the removal truck to see their new neighbors. At the same time a birdcage made by Berry-Berry in the eighth grade was smashed, and Annabel frightened the children by scolding the removal men and, absent-mindedly, handing the smashed birdcage instead of a marshmallow to a young boy. The broken birdcage symbolizes a bird that has flown but also the broken character of Annabel as she tries to cope with the absence of her eldest child.

Obsessed by notebooks, in which he records overheard conversations and copies the contents of his mother's letters, Clinton (or Clint) is considered by the neighborhood as psychologically unbalanced. The fact that at fourteen he was never seen attending high school offered further evidence of a serious disorder. The neighbors did not know that Annabel also thought her son strange, that she worried constantly about his excessive nail biting and smoking and contemplated the services of a psychiatrist. Like Arthur, who spends his youth in the basement in an attempt to escape the humdrum life of his parents, Clinton could often spend all day in his bedroom writing and daydreaming of days hanging around the old neighborhood where he was born. Much of this behavior has been caused by his brother's absence and the feeling of having been left behind, but it is also a result of "the thing that pranced around inside him" (26): the same rites of passage from adolescence to manhood, from virginity to sexual awareness, that also engulf similar characters of the period, such as Holden Caulfield in J. D. Salinger's *The Catcher in the Rye* (1951).

Indeed those two protagonists share many characteristics. They both grieve for a missing or, in Holden's case, dead brother; their mothers are overprotective and neurotic; they feel sickened by the phoniness of an adult world and experience sadness at the inevitability of joining it; and they both lack genuine friends. While Holden wanders around Manhattan alone, Clinton "would go downtown on the streetcar and sit on the steps of the City Hall where old men fed pigeons, or out in front of the Library . . . Aloha Sweet Shop . . . Voitek's Dependable Pharmacy . . . two chain drug stores . . . a chillie-con-carne place, a magazine store, and the White Tower [hamburger place]" (39). Holden, the first-person narrator of *The Catcher in the Rye,* is encouraged by a psychiatrist to translate his feelings and thoughts into words. Perhaps the thinking is that one arrives at an understanding of the seemingly incomprehensible through writing. Clinton's notebooks certainly reflect that psychology, and they illustrate the profound influence that *The Catcher in the Rye* had on Herlihy's writing at this time.

The notebooks, which often take over from the frame narrator, are a powerful part of the structure of *All Fall Down* that Herlihy would use again in his last book, *The Season of the Witch.* Like Holden's narrative, they capture a teenager's view of the world, and their poignancy and naivety contribute to the novel's sometimes-comic portrayal of family life. The notebooks also represent an adolescent turning inward, as he feels unable to talk to his parents about their loss because they cannot seem to discuss it at length. Theirs is a family composed of three private worlds polarized around an absent center, Berry-Berry: "They wouldn't go crazy, but they might continue to languish for another couple of years, or forty. Ralph in the basement, Annabel on the first floor, himself on the second, in the kind of haunted silence, broken only by occasional lies and hollow half-talk, that had filled so much of the past"

(159). As individuals they are desperately lonely. Ralph, aware of Annabel's eavesdropping on the basement, manipulates his conversation with Clinton. It is rare that Ralph actually listens to his wife, but that may be because Annabel's speech is often fragmented, shaped by a sense of panic and bordering on hysteria: "there seemed to be no part of her life that was whole, without gaps." It is true that the only "perfect listener" is Clinton, but ironically that listening merely feeds his habit for obsessively collecting material for his notebook (33, 29).

If the Williamses appear to their neighbors as a grotesque version of suburban normality, their house completes the picture:

> It is known that in every neighborhood in the United States there is at least one house that is special. Special because it is haunted, or because of an act of violence that took place there. Or there are thought to be crazy persons living in it. Or Communists. Or someone in it is thought to have served a jail term. . . . The Williams's house is big. It is made of wood. No architect had anything to do with the designing of it. Some big development organization in the twenties turned out more than a hundred just like it; so there is nothing unusual about the place. But if you were to believe a fraction of the stories that were told, the house might take on a peculiar look, even the bushes out front would seem different: children claim they bear poison flowers in the spring. (11)

Its appearance reflects both the reality of suburban housing and an architecture that would not be out of place in the nineteenth-century gothic narratives of Edgar Allan Poe. In the above passage, however, the grotesque exists only in the collective imagination of a postwar neighborhood that had become suspicious of outsiders and paranoid about difference. If the grotesque is characterized by the uncanny sense of a haunting, then there is also evidence of its existence within the family. Clinton, for instance, finds such a big house with its empty bedrooms "creepy" (21). The feeling is echoed by his father: "I think we did wrong to move in here. It's a barn, all those rooms. . . . It's almost spooky up there. All you can hear is the clock and the goddamned refrigerator" (25). Empty rooms spell empty lives. By combining the iconography of the haunted house with the noise from one of the period's best-selling consumer durables, *All Fall Down* uses the gothic to question the normality of American domestic experience. To be alive in it, said Herlihy, "is a gothic experience. . . . Wherever the eye falls there is the grotesque."[4]

Like Blount in McCullers's *The Heart Is a Lonely Hunter* (1940), whose belief in communism makes him stand out from the norms of his society,

Ralph is a political anomaly. Given that Ralph was proud of his political debating skills in the 1930s, his silence on ideological issues is particularly telling. Annabel, who also used to discuss socialism when they both met during the Depression, now "looked at him blankly, as if she had not heard a word he said" (37). The fact that this silence is wrapped up with their marriage, having children, and moving into a middle-class suburban world is particularly revealing. To preach subversive politics during this period was a dangerous and "un-American" activity. It is also symptomatic of how small individuals felt in a country that had become a global superpower in a cold-war climate. Indeed, "there had been talk of the possibility of a colossal new war; Clinton wondered if its beginning was now being announced" (38). When the family is faced with a third world war, silence is indicative of the weakness and vulnerability of the American individual at midcentury and also shapes a literary focus turning its gaze from the social sphere to the emotional world of the protagonists.

There are roughly three key episodes in the novel's structure: Clinton's trip to Key Bonita to search for his brother; Echo O'Brien's friendship with the family (which includes the return of Berry-Berry); and the death of Echo O'Brien in a car accident. Each of these episodes is fundamental in the development of Clinton from an adolescent to a man. The first episode certainly parallels the gothic description of the family home. After Berry-Berry's telegram asking Ralph for two hundred dollars so that he can buy into a fishing business, Clinton (now sixteen years of age) decides to travel to Key Bonita to join his brother. However, as Ralph shows by pointing at the atlas, Key Bonita is the farthest island off Florida's west coast. In Clinton's mind the island, connected to the mainland only by a single bridge and a bus every two days, "sounded like the most far-away place in this country." Oddly, given her possessiveness of her sons, Annabel does not appear worried at the thought of Clinton's trip. Rather she is "tickled pink" at the prospect and gives him a photograph of herself for Berry-Berry, enacting what Jayne D. Mack believes is "her high school romance fantasy" (66). The journey is an escape from an overbearing mother as much as it is a quest for a missing brother, and it is invested with the conventional ingredients—a strange landscape, the corruption of innocence, and the potential for brutality and death—of the gothic voyage.

Clinton's journey begins by bus, which takes him as far as the coast of Naples, Florida. From there he tries his hand at hitchhiking and, not having much luck, decides to walk the remaining four miles to the island. At this point the landscape becomes noticeably darker and more sinister:

> The road was straight and dreary, lined with mangroves and scrubby sea-grape trees. Serpents lived there, camouflaged in the mangroves' twisted roots, and on the surface of the dead-still waters, mosquitoes in their millions bred millions more. These bloodthirsty nuisances raised welts on Clinton's skin. . . . Scuffling lizards made nightmare noises, and frogs croaked in their hiding places. . . . The full moon, like some demon skilled in chiaroscuro, made awful shadow creatures to hide imperfectly in the foliage. Clinton wondered why he was not afraid of them: it was as if he had died and gone to hell and found it curiously to his taste. He tingled with the excitement of this terrible place. If one of the moon's monsters had come forward, he might have reached out to it eagerly, hugged it to his itching, perspiration-drenched body, and begged it to make love to him. For he had become, to himself, one of its miserable creatures, a shape of evil, ready to surrender. (69)

The passage is certainly overwritten, but it does convey the eeriness of the world that Clinton is entering. Like the Williamses' house—rumored to be "haunted" and "creepy," with a garden full of "poison flowers"—the approach to Key Bonita has a nightmarish quality, one that envelops the body and mind of the traveler. Its full moon and shadows, hidden demons and monsters are similar in atmosphere and setting to the southern gothic stories of Flannery O'Connor. While O'Connor seeks to awaken her misfits to some truth about themselves or human nature in general, Herlihy also exposes all his major characters to experiences that will alter the way they think about and conduct their lives.

After an hour or two of walking, Clinton's premonition of a motorcycle, which had passed by a few moments earlier, returning to offer him a lift proves sound, and he eventually finds himself standing in the main street of Key Bonita. One cannot help but notice that the town is in disrepair: its white wooden houses have become discolored through age and neglect; gardens resemble jungles; philodendron vines have swallowed up walls and fences; and the roots of rubber trees have sprung up through sidewalks. Unlike Seminary Street, with its uniform mowed lawns and concreted driveways, its rituals of everyday suburban life, Gasparilla Street, resembling the New Orleans of Tennessee Williams's *A Streetcar Named Desire* (1947), is a wild place in all respects: "You see people on the streets all night long. Sailors alone and in twos and threes. Latin dandies in pleated shirts, black-haired women at their elbows, drunken shrimpers clinging to parking meters for support. And all the solitary persons. Men and women young and old lean on storefronts and street lamps, wander in and out of taverns, all of them seeming to take part in the same slow and indifferent search. And for every person you see, you will feel as sharply the presence of several invisible souls. For the town is plainly haunted. Lazy ghosts of old inhabitants rock for ever on all the empty porches, and others watch over the street from shutters at second-story windows" (72). In all this Clinton cannot find his brother. Berry-Berry has checked out of his room in the Tin Pot Arms Hotel and left town. Despite being told by police lieutenant Ramírez to catch the next day's bus back to Naples and then return home, Clinton walks into the Festival Night Club. It is here that he meets a thirty-something "angel-whore" called Shirley (81).

Like Echo O'Brien, Shirley is one of the most important figures in the novel. She not only comes to play a key part in Clinton's rites of passage between adolescence and manhood but also offers a way into a deeper psychological realm that the narrative is attempting to tap. Despite being a prostitute, her room at the Tin Pot Arms Hotel seems a haven from the ugliness and corruption of the town. Here, while Clinton sleeps on the bed dreaming about Berry-Berry, she smokes a pipe of marijuana and daydreams about her dead kid brother, Willy. It seems that after her parents died, both brother and sister lived in a series of foster homes in numerous Kentucky towns. Perhaps to comfort him, she told a story about them one day growing wings and flying off together. But, tragically, Willy saw the fantasy as fact and jumped out of a tree believing his arms were wings. Blaming herself for his death, Shirley ran away from the foster home and ended up eventually in Key Bonita. Her dream, though, offers another version of events: "Except in the dream, him and me both, we just fly all over the country together, we go whippin' right through the air to North Dakota and Delaware and Greece. Even Colorado and Panama City. And we stop on various trees to rest and sing songs" (89).

What matters here is the shared nature of both dreams that, for the first time, enables Clinton to connect with another human being. They spend much of the night dancing, confessing "profound thoughts and deep secrets," and dedicating their songs to "the ghosts of all the children who had ever died or grown up in the world." Their newfound friendship culminates in sex and the loss of Clinton's virginity: "When Clinton's body had entered hers, there was a moment of perfect stillness in which he prayed for death, an end of time. But this stillness gave place to motion, and the motion repeated itself again and again, and soon they had created a subtle rhythm of closeness and pleasure, closeness and pleasure, closeness and pleasure, until there was no lavender bed spread, no bed at all, no room, no hotel, no island, no earth. Only this closeness" (92).

Clearly sex as well as companionship has the power to heal, or establish a temporary respite against grief and loss, and this understanding permeates Herlihy's fiction. Without intimacy all his characters remain bereft and isolated, vulnerable to a sense of spiritual emptiness, impotence, and madness. Where would Arthur be without Ernie; the Williamses without Echo O'Brien? It is almost impossible to picture Joe Buck apart from Rico Rizzo in *Midnight Cowboy* or Gloria separated from the commune in *The Season of the Witch*. "A person is born in the grips of this hunger for closeness," the narrator of *All Fall Down* admits; "he seldom achieves it and never can keep it for long, but he learns to be grateful for a let-up in the hunger itself, even when the let-up is brief" (92).

There is, however, circumstantial evidence that Ramírez had somehow been the voyeuristic witness of the night's events. The reader is aware of his watching the two characters as they go into the hotel, and he enters the room the next day in order to put Clinton on the bus back to Naples. Clinton realizes that there is something strange in Ramírez, "some puzzling emotion" that he "tried to suppress" (97). Nothing is explained at this point, but the reader finds out later about the lieutenant's impotence and his fascination with watching others have sex. This would mean, of course, that Shirley was somehow party to this arrangement, and we notice her looking at Clinton "almost guiltily, from the corner of her eye" (83). She is, after all, a "little girl [who] had become an old woman, her eyes cold and remote, filled with bitter, costly wisdom" (95). Innocence and its corruption are never far from Herlihy's world, and his most desperate characters, prostitutes, drug addicts, or losing gamblers learn to do grotesque things in order to survive.

It never becomes clear whether Clinton is ever fully aware of that possibility, and he returns home to Seminary Street without finding Berry-Berry. But he does now carry a vague sense of his brother's violent tendencies, as Shirley had handed him a newspaper article detailing the stabbing of her friend, and he had a feeling at the back of his mind that "he himself was part of Berry-Berry's garbage" (81). Arriving at this awareness has been emotionally taxing, and he is put to bed by Annabel in a state of deliriousness. From this point, and to the frustration of his mother, who is desperate for news of Berry-Berry, Clinton remains in bed for much of the summer. Thus begins one of the novel's most darkly comic episodes. After two weeks Annabel's impatience begins to show, and in an attempt to encourage Clinton to leave his bedroom, she stops doting on him: she brings him basic rather than fancy meals; she is late with the newspaper; and she does not respond immediately to his calls. She is aware that his malady is not all it seems, but what she does not realize is that her son does at certain times leave his room. During his mother's bath time, for instance, he runs around the house collecting cigarette butts from numerous ashtrays, rifles through the writing desk for any correspondence between Annabel and her friend Bernice O'Brien, makes inquiries with the airport about a trip to Tibet ("The woman said they could get him as far as Pakistan or India, but from there on he was on his own" [107]), and telephones Mildred Murphy in the old neighborhood to share the news of his catching malaria after traveling around South America.

This comedy depends on the naivety and immature imagination of the character. It provides the reader with a sense of relief from the tragedy of Shirley's life established in the previous episode. However, any respite is temporary, as its comedy serves also to heighten Clinton's increasing isolation and apathy: "He began vaguely to realize that he was in a kind of trap; but there seemed to be no will-power in him, and he could not concentrate on figuring a way out of it" (105). His notebook, a symptom of both this anxiety and the inner contemplation sometimes associated with gothic characters, plays a key part in investing the comedy with a darker, more tragic edge. The slippage is evident in a draft suicide note Clinton writes while in bed:

> Dear Ralph and Annabel,
>
> I suppose this news will come as a shock, but I have just killed myself and am now lying in the upstairs bathtub. . . . It is certainly not that I did not have a wonderful life with such two parents. I am merely miserable for private reasons and have been meditating in my room on these matters. It is now clear that I must go on to invisible experiences such as one has in deep dreaming, so do not think of me as dead in any way in spite of the mess in the bathroom which may tempt you to believe otherwise. Which incidentally I have also heard of the Fire Department being called in such cases as this.
>
> Your ever loving son and offspring,
> Clinton Williams I (109, 110)

It is clear that Herlihy employs the notebook as confessional in order to move *All Fall Down* away from an objectivity that limits the development of characterization in *Blue Denim*. Suicide and comedy certainly appear to be grotesque bedfellows, though very much a part of the psychology of contemporary characters such as Holden Caulfield, and their juxtaposition is one of the devices, alongside dreams, that enable the reader to catch a glimpse of the character's deepest feelings: "I picked up this notebook," Clinton confesses, "and held it like a little baby holds a teddy bear and I cried. Now I feel better. But boy did

I cry there for a while. Now I'm kind of laughing. I feel sorry for all the people who do not have a really close friend like this notebook" (67).

Down on paper the idea of suicide "is just too creepy and would probably bring on heart attacks or worse" (110). The spark that begins to awaken Clinton's curiosity, though, is the news revealed in the reading of his mother's letters from Bernice about the impending visit of her daughter, Echo O'Brien. In fact the correspondence between the two women, who became closest friends while at high school, serves a similar purpose as the notebook. Bernice suffers from obesity and arthritis and as a result is confined to a wheelchair. To write means pain, but she remains Annabel's "special confidante" (31). To Bernice, she feels able to broach her feelings about Berry-Berry, Ralph's drinking, Clinton's absence from school, and a general disaffection for life. Indeed a sexual frustration is also revealed, as she talks of "very romantic dreams" about Arch Roper, another friend from high school: "So you see I am an old middle-aged woman who still has dreams of taking walks and dating and everything" (32). Clinton's obsession with secretly reading these letters, as "Annabel wrote the truth," can be understood as his means of actually connecting with and knowing his mother. Bernice replies with advice, predictions about the future, and her concern with Echo, her only daughter and helper.

Echo is surely one of Herlihy's most beautiful characters. At the time of her visit to the Williams home, she is thirty-one years of age and lonely without friends or a lover. Taking care of her mother has meant being without a career, but she does have a particular skill in maintaining her beloved 1929 Dodge touring car. After Bernice employs a part-time helper, Echo is free to take up an invitation to visit the Williams family. Her entrance onto Seminary Street startles the neighbors, as it confronts them with a spectacle of sublime otherness: "Now all of these people looked on with respect and awe as a magnificent old automobile rolled importantly into view and came to a smooth stop in front of the Williams's house. Polished to a flawless black, this stately car, high and proud and long, with its dignified fenders and long rubber-carpeted running boards, made other cars on the street seem frivolous with their weird balloon shapes and all-day sucker colors. Eccentric only by reason of age and size, this strange car, with accents of silver glistening in the spokes of its wheels, its bumpers and headlights, gave an impression of overwhelming elegance" (114–15).

Like her car, Echo is not the product of a postwar suburban conformity but a free and genuine individual. As such, her difference represents a force for change, an example of how the Williamses could live their lives. Her attention to another person, her engagement with the world around her, begins to draw each character from his/her self-absorbed state. Naturally Clinton develops an instant crush on Echo, but so does the rest of the family. Annabel, for instance, is filled with a newfound confidence and sense of fun by their "real girl talk" (123); the basement is transformed into an intimate setting as Echo leads Clinton and his mother down the steps to play card games with Ralph.

The almost-supernatural aura Echo exudes perpetually attracts the gaze of Clinton. As the card game continues, for instance, he "watched her more closely than ever" (184). His concentration remains on her face, which for Clinton gives off a certain message. This fixation continues throughout the novel. For example, we witness Clinton "studying his brother," and on one occasion both brothers look at each other for a long time "hoping to get some clue to whatever it was that was unspoken" (157, 156). What is interesting here is that we are told by Echo that Bernice, her mother, is fascinated by phrenology, which studies the structure of the face. This gazing becomes a substitute for notebooks and dreams, but they aim to achieve the same end—that is, the attempt to see the truth of the person beyond the superficial grotesque that cannot be uttered in middle-class domestic life. So Bernice's view of Ralph after seeing his face in a photograph is that he is a genius. But when Ralph asks about Berry-Berry, Echo's reply is telling: "Oh, Uh-huh. Well, it was all kind of complicated. Some-times Mamma gets astrology mixed into it. Now I've got to concentrate. I'm black, right?" (186). Echo is not a practiced liar, unlike Berry-Berry, and her untruth only thinly masks a truth that can only bring problems later in the novel—that Berry-Berry, even deep down, is a character out to do harm.

As Echo returns home with an invitation to visit the following weekend, Clinton, for the first time, displays a positive attitude and conviction that "tomorrow, I'm going to get a job, maybe at a car-wash place" (127). In addition Ralph starts selling real estate again. It is during this summer, though, that Bernice's prediction of Berry-Berry's returning home comes true. In truth, the prediction of a Christmas return was a bit off. At the time it caused Annabel to spend her weeks neurotically writing shopping lists, baking cookies and cakes into the night, accumulating a mass of presents and cards, and, strangely, "dressing for a lover" (44). When Berry-Berry fails to show, Ralph, frustrated with the capitalist indulgence of Christmas, invites three tramps to share in the family's hospitality. Furious at the thwarting of her plans, Annabel gives each tramp ten dollars to leave, turning them symbolically into the "three departing kings" of the Nativity (51). Although the promised son does not appear, he does telephone from Covington, Kentucky, where he has been jailed for damage to a pinball machine and the stabbing of a prostitute. The prodigal son does eventually come home during the week after Echo's first visit to Seminary Street. While she represents a dream of a better future, though, his return brings with it a particular destructiveness. As Clinton discovers, his brother is a pimp, a co-owner of a brothel, a heavy drinker, and a violent abuser of women.

The scene of Berry-Berry's return also reveals a perverse relationship with his mother: "Berry-Berry and Annabel looked at each other for a long moment, a glistening look of suspension in the eyes of each of them; and then the son moved briskly forward and placed his arms about his mother. His face was buried for a moment in her hair, and then, suddenly, with an abruptness that was awkward, almost harsh, like the result of some crazy impulse, he kissed her full on the mouth. And for a moment so brief that it hardly existed at all, Clinton forgot who the man was. And he forgot who the woman was" (132–33).

Clinton's disbelief and uncertainty of what is happening must be shared by the reader. There is "muted incest" here that estranges us from the usual spectacle of mother-son relationships.[5] Indeed masculine sexuality is rarely depicted as healthy in *All Fall Down*. Suggestions of incest and rape are juxtaposed with the impotence of Echo's heavy drinking and, as it turns out, suicidal boyfriend who returned from the war "out of commission, you know what I mean?"; Lieutenant Ramírez's incapability "of any direct participation in the sexual act"; and Ralph's withdrawal from the company of his wife (121, 146). Although the reader is never told why, Berry-Berry hates his mother, hates her with a vengeance, and this seems to play a significant part in the character's downward spiral into a life of crime. As in Flannery O'Connor's "A Good Man Is Hard to Find" (1955), the family is never safe when portrayed in gothic writing and always appears on the edge of being pulled apart by malignant forces. But as much as the scene exposes that possibility, it also offers a glimmer of hope with the approaching weekend and the return of the healing, angelic-like presence of the virgin Echo O'Brien.

For all its associations with paranoia and teenage rebellion, American suburban life of the 1950s is often remembered nostalgically. Summers are an important part of that image: the first holiday romance; the family barbeque on the front lawn; children polishing their father's car in the driveway or learning to ride a bike. It is a picture of innocence, a haven against the uncertainties of the world and a changing American society. *All Fall Down* reproduces that picture, as Echo's ever-optimistic and energetic presence help to reconnect the familial ties of the Williams family. From morning to evening the house is filled with the buzz of friendly chatter and stories around the breakfast table; smells of homemade apple pies fill the air; and going for walks and picnics in the country is the order of the day. During this time Berry-Berry, who has not returned to his brothel, and Echo, who is very much a member of the family, become a couple, and Annabel and Ralph find a renewed tolerance for each other. However, summers end, and Clinton stumbles on two revelations: the first is that Echo takes medicine to calm her nerves; the second is that she is pregnant with his brother's baby. Eavesdropping on their conversation in the basement late one night, almost a mirror of Annabel's listening to Ralph, Clinton understands an important fact about Berry-Berry: that he cannot declare love and take the responsibility of caring for another human being. Distressed at the breakup, Echo drives home to Toledo in a heavy storm and dies instantly as her car veers off the road and ploughs into the home of a country dentist.

News of her death has two important consequences. The first is the decision by Clinton to drive over to the brothel at the edge of town, climb the stairs to Berry-Berry's bedroom, take the gun out of the bottom drawer of the cupboard, and shoot his brother dead. The form of the narrative changes during part of this episode to expose the unconscious of the character caught in the insanity of conflict and rage. The voice inside his head tells Clinton to wait in a dimly lit chair in the corner of the room and then watch his brother with one of his prostitutes. What he sees and hears is shocking:

BERRY-BERRY: Help me. Help me.
THE WOMAN: There, baby, now just lay back and rest. Will you do that for Mamma?
BERRY-BERRY: Don't leave me, don't leave.
THE WOMAN: I wouldn't leave you, baby. Mamma's here.
BERRY-BERRY: Lie down with me.
THE WOMAN: What makes you want to hurt Mamma? Please, sweetheart. You want to put your hand there? All right, baby, put your hand there.
BERRY-BERRY: Are you Annabel?
THE WOMAN: That's right, baby; I'm Annabel. (212)

Clinton finally realizes that his brother is not the romantic hero figure he has been missing but rather a human being capable of grotesque and horrific acts. It is that realization that takes Clinton into the deepest and most profound dreams of the novel.

In dealing with the emotional and psychological baggage of his characters, dreams are a fundamental part of Herlihy's deepening narrative perspective. They convey to the reader an essential uninhibited truth of conflicts within the characters and certain nuances of plot. Indeed, Mack offers an interesting understanding of Herlihy's use of dreams. In one respect they help to mask particular problems that have been caused by the absence of intimacy and love, such as Ralph's nostalgia for his socialist life in the 1930s, Annabel's imagined romance with Arch Roper, and Shirley's dream of flying over the world with her dead brother. They are daydreams that reveal desperation and loneliness at their heart. But there are other dreams that represent signposts for the development and maturity of an adolescent character and have the potential to offer solutions to seemingly insurmountable conflicts. As he sits with a gun in Berry-Berry's room in the brothel, Clinton's dream conforms wholeheartedly to the latter. His mind wanders to an elevated position from where he can notice the fragility and smallness of his brother's house:

> In the surrounding trees of this vast orchard, perched high on all the naked limbs, were tens of thousands of people, all children, and all singing. All of the people he knew or had ever known were in the branches and he recognized them, even Annabel and Ralph, but now they were child people. Each person, of these tens of thousands, sang his individual song, each one separate, different; and it was impossible to make out the words or melodies. Heard from so great a height, all of them together made one sound that was like the wind. But then the wind itself came along, and it made no sound at all. It crept in from all sides, invisible and silent. Clinton knew there was no way to warn anyone of the approach of a menace that could be neither seen nor heard; therefore he had no choice but to witness whatever might take place. So the wind blew, and it blew with such force that all the branches of all the trees, even the highest ones, began to shake so violently that all of the tiny singers were blown away. The branches were bare and silent again and there were no children left in the world. (213–14)

Like Holden Caulfield's dream of trying to catch children falling over a cliff, Clinton's has witnessed a prophetic vision of the inevitability of adulthood. The "solution," though, does not lie in just that but also in the existential recognition that each person is an individual responsible for his own path in life and the garden he keeps. Once he recognizes that, he can feel the release of a deep emotional outpouring that signals his passage to manhood.

During Clinton's dream Berry-Berry also has a moment of revelation. As he wakes up and sees his brother with a gun, he realizes the terrible truth of the situation. This forces Berry-Berry to experience a raft of various emotions, including self-hatred, emptiness, and an acknowledgment of his deep love for his brother. Bending down to touch his brother's skin, "he knew instantly, and in a way that he had never known before, that there is life in other people than himself, blood and spirit, vulnerability, a heartbeat, a pulse." The painful lesson is finally learned, but it is too late to recapture love for his kid brother because, as he notices, Clinton had turned into "a mysterious giant possessed of powers that he had little hope of attaining" (216, 217).

Arthur Miller argued that there is a great optimism in literary tragedy because it teaches an important lesson to those who are left alive after the death of the hero. His most famous protagonist, Willy Loman, is elevated to a tragic status because his son, Biff, who saw his father as "a dime a dozen," comes to see him as "a prince."[6] Similarly, Clinton, who originally thought of Echo as a middle-aged virgin, eventually recognizes her as a "royal figure" (200). While Willy's death shows the Loman family the problems of contemporary American society, the lessons drawn from Echo's death are more personal. For Annabel and Ralph, it means an attempt to try again at their marriage. It means Annabel's giving up her infatuation with her son. For Clinton, now a young man, it means a radical alteration of his attitude to life and the following of Echo's attitude as a philosophy: "In fact, the kind of person I believe I am now, is the kind that when somebody *else* has a nightmare, then I wake them up and take care of them—the kind of person that puts my arms around them and says, 'It's ok, honey, everything's going to be ok now. It's only the wind'" (224).

All Fall Down represents a seminal text in Herlihy's developing literary aesthetic. The breakdown of families and the complexities of adolescent experience continue to occupy his interest. It is the world of personal experience, shaped by the social context of mid-century America, that underpins this focus. Herlihy's question "Do you think American life produces more grotesques per capita than other societies do"[7] to his friend Lyle Bongé reveals the gothic influence permeating his novel. Characters' dreams, and other forms of reflection, help us to understand this influence as a means to penetrate the emotional and psychological baggage of characters. In that, *All Fall Down* succeeds where *Blue Denim* fails. But it would take his next novel, *Midnight Cowboy,* to bring this style to the attention of a mass readership.

CHAPTER 5

Midnight Cowboy

Midnight Cowboy (1965) is Herlihy's most famous novel, due in no small part to John Schlesinger's Oscar-winning movie of the same title. The novel continues Herlihy's fascination with characters' emotional and psychological baggage, revealed as a means to establish a deeper and more fulfilling reconnection with the world around them. No character needs this connection more than Joe Buck. As a loner, misfit, and innocent figure, he dons the quasi-mythical costume of a cowboy and journeys from Texas to New York to seek his fortune as a hustler. The encounters he has with lonely, mixed-up, and eccentric strangers along the way are fundamental to understanding his development and maturation. Like all of Herlihy's characters, he learns something about himself and the world by leaving home. But where *Blue Denim* and *All Fall Down* expose the frailty of the suburban home in a moment of crisis, *Midnight Cowboy,* as much more of a city book, implicitly questions the nature of contemporary urban life and its impact on the health of its inhabitants.[1]

The novel is divided into three parts that could loosely be given the following subtitles: "The Preparation for the Journey to New York"; "Arrival and Survival in Manhattan"; and "The Dream of Escape to Florida." At their core is Joe Buck's emotional relationship with others and the changing perception of himself. However, in Herlihy's world emotional and psychological landscapes cannot be neatly segregated from each other. Dreams, again, are crucial devices that serve to provide an overlaying narrative structure that takes us back into the past as much as they hold us in the present and transport us into possible futures. At the heart of this structure are two continually juxtaposed and contemporary worlds: one of lonesomeness and the other a quest for emotional healing, companionship, and love.

The novel opens as Joe Buck is about to quit his job as a kitchen hand at the Sunshine Cafeteria in Houston, Texas. It is spring, a season associated with rebirth, and he feels like "a shimmering new man" (19). Looking at the reflection in the mirror of his "HTEL" room (the missing "O" in "HOTEL" indicates its state of disrepair), a fixation that he does not lose until the end of the novel, Joe sees the image of a cowboy: sexually charged, masculine, available. His newfound confidence, inspired by a fresh out-of-the-packet costume, invests a daydream of humiliating a bullying employer, taking a wad of cash that is rightfully owed him, and walking out under the watchful and respectful gaze of the customers. The sequence relies on the myth of the western hero propagated by a postwar cinema that featured the likes of Gary Cooper, James Stewart, and Alan Ladd as invincible gunslingers who righted wrongs before riding off into the sunset. It is a quintessentially American phenomenon that the cowboy carries to New York. As Herlihy says: "I thought that all Americans were riding into town at high noon, casting NO shadow at all, zealous after their own purities, and being caught short at midnight."[2]

But Joe is no Shane. In truth he is unable to confront the manager of the cafeteria about wages owed and instead leaves as quietly as possible with only a few words to a middle-aged man washing dishes. Here we begin to see the emergence of a pattern to the novel, which juxtaposes the external landscape of reality with the internal world of imagination and dreams. As much as his cowboy persona communicates masculine power and confidence, it also thinly masks the hero's profound sense of insecurity. He is, then, an American product: driven by a dynamism that enables him to invent himself anew and a foresight that moves him to realize his dreams but at the same time haunted by a fear that "he might easily wreck it all by weeping" (7). As he walks out of the diner, his perspective of the town fades before a mental vision of himself walking down Park Avenue, where "rich ladies looking out their windows swooned to see a cowboy" (10). The next thing we know, he is about to step into a Greyhound bus, destination New York. Like Jack Kerouac's Beat classic *On the Road* (1957) and other narratives of the road-book genre, *Midnight Cowboy* sends its protagonist on a pilgrimage of self-discovery.

At the beginning of this pilgrimage, the narrative alters its perspective to offer a fuller context surrounding Joe's life, which reminds the reader that baggage carried in the unconscious shapes the character's view of external events. In Herlihy's works the families seem caught in a perpetual state of breakdown and crisis that can, at least in the novels, lead to some form of resolution. *Midnight Cowboy* is no exception to that pattern. Joe was brought up during the war by three blonde prostitutes and without any sign of a father. After a time he ends up with his grandmother Sally Buck in Albuquerque,

New Mexico. In a notable performance in Schlesinger's film, Brenda Vaccaro captures the essence of a grandmother who cares more for drinking and courting numerous rancherlike beaus than taking responsibility for the care of a young boy. But one of these beaus, another western figure, Woodsy Niles, becomes a kind of surrogate father for a time, before leaving like the others. During that time Joe began to feel like a cowboy.

Left on his own, his constant watching of TV leads to a blurring of the boundaries between fantasy and reality. Inevitably that leads to a fixation with the TV cowboy, one of the more iconographic figures of the immediate postwar era, "riding high in his saddle, face against the sun, jaw squared toward goodness and justice, bursting with his own hardness and strength and purpose" (18). The phallic nature of that image—with its key words "riding high . . . bursting . . . hardness"—is beyond question. The fact that this takes place immediately prior to Joe's sudden awareness that he "inhabited the body of a man" is crucial for understanding the genesis of a sexual identity and costume that he ends up wearing during his new life as a hustler (19). Indeed there is a slippage between the world of the western genre—with its blonde female characters who populated "every stagecoach and covered wagon, every saloon and every general store"—and the reality of being brought up by four blonde women (18). This certainly shapes Joe's attraction to blonde-haired characters such as Rico Rizzo and Hansel and Gretel McAlbertson, whom he meets on the streets of New York. The fact that he considers these particular characters "kin" or "his children" suggests that "blonde" is a semiotic of home and family, a dream for which he is unwittingly striving (258, 206).

While wandering around the streets of Albuquerque, a lonely boy of seventeen, he meets Anastasia Pratt. She is one of Herlihy's most troubled and abused adolescent characters. Whereas Arthur escapes into the basement in *Blue Denim* and Clinton escapes into his notebook in *All Fall Down,* Anastasia withdraws from life by allowing others to use her body for sexual gratification. Indeed she has been providing this service since the age of twelve. All this is a shock to her parents—"the father a strict, hard-working, irritable bank cashier and the mother a thin-lipped, shifty-eyed piano player at the Truth Church" (23)—who seem, like the Major and Jessie or Annabel and Ralph in the above-discussed books, to be stereotypes of disgruntled members of middle-class family life. Anastasia is also "ordinary" (22): a fifteen-year-old girl whose virginal appearance and teenage clothes, ankle socks, saddle oxfords, and the odd dab of makeup do not distinguish her as in any way special or different.

Perhaps Anastasia's behavior is caused by the sense of being simply ordinary and by seeing adult role models who have resigned themselves to quiet unhappiness, as is the case with all of Herlihy's other main characters. She sees something equally lonely and innocent in Joe, and for one summer when school is out, they become young lovers. Eventually, however, her reputation is exposed, and her committal in an insane asylum signals another end to a relationship and her absence from the novel. Anastasia plays an important part in Joe's development as a character. Through her he loses his virginity and, though not exactly in love, begins to feel some sense of caring for "her terrible lonesomeness" (31). Schlesinger's film does more with the lasting effects of this relationship. Alone in Manhattan, John Voight's Joe is haunted by an echo of Anastasia's voice—"You're the only one Joe, the only one"—and a nightmare scenario in which during sex they are separated by the authorities. The novel details only the immediate effects of this separation, which results in Joe's feeling worthless and ever more bereft.

With the frequent absence of Joe's grandmother, Anastasia represents his quest for an "alliance with someone" (32). With Anastasia gone, that quest becomes increasingly more intense and diverse. Joe's feeling of emptiness is filled, temporarily, by fleeting sexual encounters as he begins to take on the principles that shaped the tragic life of Anastasia. But something else is revealed here: a subtle but revealing gay subtext that exists in all of Herlihy's novels. Bobby Desmond, who has always treated Joe with a certain respect, enters the picture for a brief moment. Taking him for rides in his car, buying a six-pack of beer to share, Bobby "wanted the experience of being used by Joe in the same way Anastasia Pratt had been used by him that night in the storeroom of the World." Joe "gave the young man the experience he wanted" but did so in the hope of some permanent companionship (33). However, three weeks later Bobby gets married and Joe is left alone once more.

It is in this state of lonesomeness that Joe passively "drifts into his twenties" (33) and eventually, at twenty-three years of age, gets conscripted into the army. Here he learns of his grandmother's death, caused by her falling from a horse while trying to impress a new beau. His intense grief, combined with the panic of being totally alone in the world, leads to a dream that becomes a recurring and fundamental feature of *Midnight Cowboy:*

> One night he dreamed a dream . . . of an endless chain of people marching across the side of the world. From his vantage point in some chill and dark and silent corner he could see them coming up from over the eastern

> horizon, all joined at the bellybutton by a golden rope of light and walking to a rousing march beat, and he could see them moving along until they had gone out of sight behind the western horizon. There were people of all kinds, bus drivers, musicians, and soldiers and ten-cent store girls; there were Chinamen and pilots, hillbillies and fat men and red-headed women; you could find miners and bank clerks there, millionaires and store detectives, swamis, babies, grandmothers, thieves; look for any kind of person in the golden rope and there would be one, a whore, a dwarf, a saint, a crazy man, cop, teacher, reporter, pretty girl, bookkeeper, shortstop, ragpicker. There seemed to be every type of person but his own. He made many attempts to join them, running up close to the marching stream of people, hoping to discover an opening big enough to slip into; but just as he would find one there would be a rapid closing of ranks, the chain would become tight and exclusive and impossible to break into, and the dreamer was forced to remain always on this chill and dark and silent edge. (37–38)

As Jayne D. Mack correctly observes, this first image of the golden rope represents a problem dream in that it reflects Joe's search for, and inability to find, a sense of belonging.[3] As in *All Fall Down,* where Clinton unconsciously adapts Shirley's dream of her dead brother into a prophetic vision that signals togetherness and maturity, the problem dream signals a quest for a resolution that includes companionship, a caring for others, and love.

The quest begins with Joe's move to Houston. In search of an acquaintance from the army, Joe stumbles on the Sunshine Cafeteria, where he will eventually work as a kitchen hand. This is the kind of all-night diner one sees in Edward Hopper's painting *Nighthawks* (1942): a gathering place for people without any purpose in life and with no other place to go. It is a site for the lost and the lonely, "that special breed known best in the U.S.A." (41). But "special breed" does not attract a description of the grotesque, as it does so evidently in *The Sleep of Baby Filbertson* or the portrayal of Key Bonita in *All Fall Down.* Rather it reflects a poignant narrative perspective that echoes Sal Paradise's experience of postwar America in Jack Kerouac's *On the Road*—as irretrievably forlorn, beaten down, lonesome.

Thus the Sunshine Cafeteria has an all-night crowd that includes "silent persons . . . solitary people . . . smoking cigarettes and staring out over empty coffee cups" (41). The loneliness masks a deeper truth that Herlihy is playing with in parts of *Midnight Cowboy.* Like the Beats' representation of a sexually diverse underground population, Herlihy's perspective reveals a semihidden homosexual world peopled by "pretty, rather sissified" young men who "dressed with a kind of ostentatious boyishness" and "seem[ed] to be suffering some nameless common loss" (42, 43, 41). Joe's naivety limits his understanding of that world, and, not for the first time, his search for a companion can be understood as an implicit quest for guidance.

Perry, a young regular at the diner, appears to step up to that role of "keeper of some remarkable secret . . . into the mysteries that lay beyond the revolving door of the Cafeteria" (47). However, although he sits with Joe night after night, his brooding silence and his prolonged stare "touched with death" make Perry one of the novel's most untrustworthy protagonists (44). His relationship with Marvin, a balding thirty-year-old whose desire to be humiliated enables Joe to understand Townsend P. Locke in part 3 of the book, shows Perry's fascination with sexual power and domination. The reader understands how far such a tendency for exploitation can go in the brothel episode, where Perry conspires with two of Herlihy's most grotesque characters. Tombaby Barefoot, "an oddly constructed halfbreed," and his mother, Juanita, "a small, middle-aged hag," secretly watch Joe have sex with a young prostitute before raping him (72, 73).

As a result of the rape, Joe locks himself in his room at the "HTEL" and, though in pain, attempts to understand his life up to that point. His realization that nobody has ever really loved him, including his grandmother, leads to a "new fury" that inspires an urgency to take care of himself (89). According to Herlihy, this, coupled with a quest for companionship, is Joe's "saving grace . . . something essential within him [that] gives him the power to be committed."[4] Ironically it is Juanita's words describing New York, as full of "fags and money and hungry women" and where a "young stud" could "clean up good," that imbue Joe with a dream of leaving Houston (80). Fueled by this ambition, he saves his wages from working at the cafeteria and begins to reflect on his newfound confidence. From a narrative perspective, this new identity represents a transition between childhood and adulthood, the same rites of passage that permeate all of Herlihy's novels. *Midnight Cowboy* situates that within an American mythical tradition: "There is an Indian legend that at a certain time in the life of a young man he is given a dream in which he sees a mask, and when he awakens he must set to work carving a real mask in that dream image." For Joe, that mask is the image of the cowboy hero, and "he must wear it into battle in order to be victorious" (93). As the novel progresses, the reader sees the broadening out of this mythical pattern.

Part 2 returns the reader to the opening pages of the novel, as Joe is now on the Greyhound bus to New York. His dream of "rope[ing] in this whole fuckin' island" shapes a view of its urban reality (100). From his window at the Times Square Palace Hotel, the sight of "a stream of early evening pedestrians" is invested with a "throbbing and rich and noisy" sexual energy of Forty-second Street (103, 100). He takes this confidence out onto Lexington Avenue, where he meets his first client, Cass Trehune. Cass, clearly in her fifties and wealthy, encourages Joe to follow her up to a penthouse apartment. But Joe's out-of-town naivety lets him down once more. After sex Cass is insulted at being asked for payment, and Joe feels compelled to give her twenty dollars to calm her hysterical outburst. This is yet another episode where the hero learns something to aid his development. An innocent eye needs an experienced hand, someone who knows the ropes and can guide one through the thicks and thins of city life. Such a character, played insightfully in the movie by Dustin Hoffman, is Rico Rizzo of the Bronx.

The peculiarity of their encounter offers a key understanding of the novel's development of plot and characterization. The following takes place after Joe has left Cass's apartment: "He walked for a while, looking at the street signs but giving no real thought to the direction he was taking. At midnight he found himself in another saloon. . . . He had to have some advice, that was all there was to it. The thought became an obsession: He wouldn't do another thing in this town until he'd found someone who knew the ropes and could give him some guidance. . . . Returning to the bar in a new frame of mind, Joe found he was being looked at by a person who had arrived in his absence. . . . 'Excuse me for starin,' he said in a New York accent, 'I was jus admirin' that colossal shirt.' . . . Without considering the matter, he [Joe] was certain this kind of speech went hand in hand with a knowledge of the underworld" (118–20). Throughout the novel Joe's passivity, a lack of any direction in life, has led to a victim's status where an experience of abandonment and exploitation is the rule. Indeed his dream of success as a hustler is continuously interrupted by the baggage of this past. The above passage at first merely serves to affirm that status as Joe's path has led him to one of the confidence tricksters who inhabit New York at night. But by the end of part 2, the fact that they have become like brothers helps us to understand that path as invested with ideas of "destiny" (98).[5]

Rico is a fascinating character, perhaps the most complex and most-loved protagonist to appear in Herlihy's body of work. Born Enrico Salvatore Rizzo to first-generation Italian Americans, he grew up in the Bronx with nine brothers and three sisters, a father who worked all hours as a bricklayer, and a bedridden mother. Rico fared no better. As a child he was struck down by several illnesses, including pneumonia and an infantile paralysis that left "his body gyrating grotesquely with each step" (157). The death of his parents—his mother, "a burnt out child bearer" (166), when he was eight years old, and his father of a heart attack eight years later—and the running away of all his siblings made Rico an orphan. Alone in the world, he began to make a life as a petty criminal on the streets of New York.

So Joe's intuition that the twenty-one-year-old Rico, or Ratso (the derogatory name by which he is known on the streets), has "a knowledge of the underworld" is correct (157). For twenty dollars he arranges for Joe to meet a high-class pimp who is able to offer lucrative jobs for hustlers. However, Mr. O'Daniel is no pimp but rather is a half-crazy street evangelist who, coincidentally, also lives in the Times Square Palace Hotel. Despite O'Daniel's eccentricities, Herlihy allows him to utter the novel's lasting statement: "You're a little different than a lot of the boys t' come to me. . . . With most of 'em, they seem to be, well, troubled, confused. . . . Well, I'll bet you got one thing in common with them other boys: I'll bet you're *lonesome!*" (134). Joe is not alone in this; all the characters in the novel, bar none, suffer from some form of loneliness, and these sentiments enable the reader to see the start of Joe's inclusion in the golden rope that connects human beings with each other.

Out on the streets and realizing the trick, Joe has a sudden fantasy of murdering Rico in front of a crowd of people. The slippage between reality and fantasy permeates *Midnight Cowboy,* as it does most of Herlihy's writing. We see it, for example, when the figure of Tombaby leaving the room in the brothel becomes in Joe's mind a figure riding out of Texas on an eight-foot stuffed giraffe. What may seem clear to the reader is the cartoonlike quality of such a fantasy. As a form of daydream, it offers a narrative perspective that goes underneath the skin of the character, exposing the truth of his unconscious feelings and the extent to which he is tied to a past of TV watching and isolation. This dream ends abruptly, though, as his eyes are drawn by a newspaper photograph of a "West Virginia mass murderer" who could "pass as a double" for Joe. The shock completely unsettles any view of himself as a cowboy, and he is left looking in the mirror "as if he had just now met himself for the first time" (140).

Unable to find Rico and thrown out of his hotel without any belongings, Joe is forced to wander "deeper and deeper into September" (149). Ironically homeless wandering becomes an educating experience.[6] He locates the city's public spaces where he can keep clean and well groomed and also finds cheap places to eat and sleep. He realizes, from watching the young hustlers on Eighth Avenue and Forty-second Street, both the need to occupy a patch and the sadness of his profession. But the most profound revelation originates in "some strange and enjoyable new view of the way in which people, even himself, were connected to the planet Earth" (152). Joe is no longer excluded in his mind from the golden rope of human existence, and this Whitmanite experience is fundamental to the stripping and rebuilding of the character's identity.[7]

The character's new experience also lends itself to a political reading of the novel by, first of all, showing the reader the poverty and destitution of America's principal city. In this political sense the island serves as a prison, "barricaded by the buildings of the steamship companies" (147). Here a sense of personal alienation and social inequality permeates every walk of life. In this atmosphere Joe questions the point of working for a living, and he eventually listens to Mr. O'Daniel's street sermon with new ears: "I have found the streets of this nation filled with lonesome people, young boys, middle-aged men, girls and women of all descriptions, all of them gripped by the bleakest solitude" (153). As one of the novel's profound truths, this signals the end of the character's three-week solitude in the city by reintroducing Rico into the narrative.

What may be less clear to the reader is "that the odds against finding Rizzo were overwhelming" (139). Indeed the coincidence of spotting him gazing out through the window of a Greenwich Village diner helps us understand *Midnight Cowboy* as a generic piece of urban fiction, conforming to particular themes and using certain devices that are important components of the genre. An almost ethnographic impulse to portray the reality of life as alienated and poor is certainly part of this and can be found in such seminal city narratives as Theodore Dreiser's *Sister Carrie* (1900) and Nelson Algren's *The Man with the Golden Arm* (1949). Indeed texts such as Paul Auster's *City of Glass* (1985) also play with the idea of coincidence and, in so doing, highlight the juxtaposition between chance and fate. Joe's reintroduction to Rico is clearly fated by the author because it continues the reawakening of Joe as a protagonist, helps to forge a sense of companionship and love, and uses the political aspect of the narrative to guide the reader further into the underworld of New York.

Although the outlaw is the "archenemy" (156) of the cowboy, Rico offers Joe the ultimate gesture of companionship—his home. This "home" is located in the empty and run-down old Puerto Rican blocks where Rico has been living since the age of sixteen. Herlihy is keen to situate it within a particular social-realist milieu: "In New York there are always a large number of tenement buildings being emptied for eventual demolition. One by one the families are moved out, and as they leave, the owner, a great corporation, has a large white X taped across each window of the evacuated space" (158). The city's postwar period had witnessed the town planner Robert Moses's destruction of numerous poor and ethnic neighborhoods to make way for offices, expressways, bridges, and, as Jane Jacobs argues, "promenades that go from no place to nowhere."[8] But as much as "X" is a sign of impending destruction, it also marks the spot on a map and makes that hidden and boarded-off world visible for the reader.

In the summer of 1990 Lyle Bongé wrote to his friend with a realization of "what a splendid thing you had done. You had taken people who were at best statistical fragments and made them real."[9] But even though the novel's realism is affirmed by transferring marginal people to center stage, by the late 1960s Herlihy had become convinced that for people to survive, the cities had to be evacuated. There is a hint of this as Joe sees the Manhattan skyline for the first time as "a crowded graveyard" (99) and by the end as a place from which to escape. This urgency becomes increasingly prominent in the final part of the novel as Joe comes to share Rico's dream of a life in Florida. For now, though, they become a common sight walking the streets of Manhattan, and for the first time in his life, Joe is happy.

In "Orpheus in New York: The Classical Descent of *Midnight Cowboy,*" Charles F. Saylor understands the novel as following the mythical narrative of Orpheus and Eurydice. This reading is persuasive on a number of levels. Orpheus, like Buck, enters the underworld to rescue Eurydice and finds a landscape, like New York, blighted by alienation, illness, and destruction. Joe's invite to "the kingdom of hell" party, which is located in Hansel and Gretel McAlbertson's "filthy loft in the northwest corner of Broadway and Harmony Street" (176), is, for Saylor, a descent that ends in Buck's ascent as an individual. Here, Mother Ceres, "an outsider from the Midwest, promotes Buck's spiritual self-rescue, or ascent, from the underworld, as did the original Ceres of her own child."[10]

As in the stories of James Purdy, the interweaving of real and classical narrative patterns that opens part 3 depends also on American myths.[11] The cowboy, the icon of the Old West, has entered the modern city and found it wanting. His friendship with the urban native Rico represents an "alliance" between old and new values and conflicting historical versions of utopian and dystopian America. With that in mind, the stairs leading to the McAlbertsons' home take on an important symbolic quality. As they enter the stairwell on their way to the party, Joe wipes the perspiration from Rico's brow. Staring at each other, "some vague, awful thing had come into evidence between them, hovering in the air between them like a skeleton" (182). Although this "thing" is never made explicit, the final word in the passage signals death. At the end of the party, Rico's fall down the stairs reflects the fall of Eurydice, as Saylor argues, but it can also be equally understood as the fall of urban America, as F. Scott Fitzgerald's narrator Nick Carraway in *The Great Gatsby* (1925) saw it, from its original idea as a garden of the New World.

Such an apocalyptic reading does not situate *Midnight Cowboy* outside an American literary preoccupation with the city. Since Herman Melville's *Bartleby the Scrivener: A Story of Wall Street* (1853), the city has represented the corruption of the American individual and his dream of freedom and prosperity. But it is curious to think that Joe's full awakening from this corruption depends on the death of Rico, just as Nick Carraway's escape from New York relies on the death of his friend Jay Gatsby. The client, "a girl in an orange dress," whom Joe picks up at the party recognizes him as "pure symbol" but also tells Rico "to get lost, *bad* lost. Y'know? Like *dead!*" (189, 192, 200). There is a struggle here between these two urban characters. Both have emotional claims on the cowboy. But Joe's rejection of Rico's demands to "Carry me" like "a damsel" (201), in order to get the money for both of them to travel to Florida, shows how far Joe has come as a strong, confident, and far-seeing knight-errant.

For all its symbolic connotations, the literal fall down the stairs exacerbates Rico's illness. When Joe returns home from a night with a client, bearing gifts paid for by the twenty-dollar fee, he finds Rico shivering in bed and unable to eat. What is worse, Rico now feels unable to walk:

> [RICO]: "I don't think I can walk." Ratso looked at the wall. He was obviously embarrassed. "I mean, I been fallin' down a lot. . . . I mean what do they, uh, you know—do with you—if you can't, uh . . . Agh, shit!"
> [JOE]: "Who? What does who do with you?"
> [RICO]: "I don't know. The cops. Or the—how should I know?"
> [JOE]: "You mean," Joe said, "like if you can't walk?"
> Ratso nodded.
> [JOE]: "Well, what's the cops got to do with that? That's none of their fucking business who walks and who don't." (209)

How should the reader understand this illness? Herlihy has certainly established a parallel between the destruction of New York and that of its native character. But the illness also prompts Joe to respond unselfishly to the needs of his friend, by reigniting Rico's idealistic dream of a life in Florida. There, in paradise, life is sweet. There is no illness because the two life-giving properties—warmth and coconuts—are in abundance. Like the Joads' migration to California in John Steinbeck's classic *The Grapes of Wrath* (1939), Rico's illness has transformed this dream of traveling to Florida as a pilgrimage where the urban native and the cowboy can be cleansed and healed.

In order to realize this vision, Joe returns to the street in a last-ditch attempt to raise fifty dollars to pay for bus tickets. Here he encounters "Townsend P. (for Pederson) Locke of Chicago ('Call me Towny')" (213).

Locke, whose name represents what Terrell Dixon calls "the jail or cage of the lonely life," is a fascinating eccentric.[12] In New York to attend a paper manufacturer's conference, he is clearly accustomed to picking up young hustlers. His constant talking, his "sick" obsession with his elderly mother who looks like Queen Victoria," their life in a "glorious tower overlooking the lake," and, as we find out, his need, like Marvin's, to be humiliated and hurt during sex help us to understand him as one of Mr. O'Daniel's lonesome Americans (219, 221). Even the city's sexual energy—"your heart goes tum-te-tum-te-tum, and the projector in that theatre goes clickety-clickety-click, and each one of those cars goes *ggggrrrrrhhhhhoooooo-mmmmmmmmmm* and oh!"—serves only to remind him how much "I loathe life, I loathe every minute of it" (227).

Understandably, Joe is in urgent need of getting paid for his time. After returning to the X flat to take Rico to the Greyhound bus terminal, where he leaves him wrapped in the mythic cover of an "Indian blanket," Joe visits Locke again to demand $50 (231). During this episode we learn that Locke is not the only character to use the encounter as a confessional, as Joe declares Rico "family goddammit, an' I got to get 'em down to Florida" (235). Although a new truth for Joe, the hard-luck story attracts little sympathy. In the violent tussle that ensues, Locke's sexual arousal almost justifies Joe's taking payment of $121. We can read this scene on two levels. First, Joe has nearly killed a man by beating him senseless, and because of this the mythical journey to paradise becomes ambiguous at best and at worst corrupt. But one could also argue, in symbolic terms, that Locke, like Rico, needed to be sacrificed, as he represented all the greed and immorality of the city, in order for the hero to move on to holier ground.

This ambiguity allows us to understand the journey to Florida as representing death at the same time as it symbolizes the promise of a new life. Without doubt the bus ride is the most moving scene of the novel and offers a resolution to the experience of lonesomeness that Joe encounters both in himself and in others: "And so here he was with this burden on his hands, responsible for the care of another person, a sickly, crippled person at that. But oddly enough, he liked the feeling it gave him. It was a curious kind of burden under which he felt lighter instead of heavier, and warm. The seat became exceptionally comfortable and his head fit the pillow better. He felt joined to everything that touched him, and pretty soon he fell asleep, dreaming his golden rope dream" (247). Joe is now part of the golden rope. After sobbing alone at a truck stop; throwing the cowboy gear in the trash and buying new clothes, unconsciously rejecting the mirror as a means to think; and, for the first time, realizing that he is capable of having a regular life, he is finally transformed into a new man: an American Adam. This new man is capable of self-sacrifice and love for another human being. But there is also a simple pragmatism that confirms Joe's new American status: "I'm going to have to go to work, I don't know, sweeping, doing dishes. . . . 'Cause we want it to be nice down there, don't we?" (246). Rico's illness is too acute for him to survive, and his fantasies of Florida are too great. His death signals the resurrection of Joe Buck.[13]

After the insularity of Herlihy's earlier published play *Blue Denim*, *Midnight Cowboy* continues to develop an aesthetic that mingles realism's devotion to external time and place with a probing of the emotional and psychological aspects of characters. The novel turns on a particular truth, once coined by the poet W. H. Auden, that "we must love one another or die."[14] The "uninhabitable" and "suffocating" nature of the city, the novel is saying, undermines the progress toward that relationship.[15] But for the cowboy Joe Buck, the encounters with the city's misfits impart a particular wisdom and fuel a self-realization that helps him mature as a caring American individual. As Herlihy believed, "We 20th-century men are learning, because we must in order to survive, that brotherhood is not an ideal but a necessity."[16] It would take another six years and a new novel for Herlihy to consider this principle on female terms.

CHAPTER 6

A Story That Ends with a Scream and Eight Others

"'My children,' said the old man to his boys, scared by a figure in the dark entry, 'my children, you will never see anything worse than yourselves.'" Ralph Waldo Emerson's words, the epigraph to *A Story That Ends with a Scream and Eight Others* (1967), convey Herlihy's continued fascination with the vulnerabilities and secrets of his characters.[1] These characters resemble a carnivalesque parade of eccentric old ladies, psychopaths, midgets, giants, and lonely housewives. They are, as one reviewer noted, "life's victims, the insulted and injured, the forlorn and alienated."[2] Moving between familiar and unfamiliar worlds, between conscious and unconscious experiences, the lives of the characters are tragic and unsettlingly comic. Set mainly in Florida, in closed-down bars, asylums, trailer parks, and motel rooms, the atmosphere is oppressively hot, tense, haunting. As psychological fables of ordinary Americana, though, these stories resist any telling resolution.

A trailer park is the setting for the title story. The gothic ingredients evident in the opening paragraph—a half moon, silhouettes of two witchlike figures, darkness momentarily illuminated by the flame of a freshly lit cigarette—hint at an emotional complexity that contrasts with the plastic and superficial nature of the trailer park. Here we are introduced to Mary Ellen McClure and her neighbor Ivy Alesandro. They are bored middle-class housewives, unfulfilled in their personal lives. Their husbands seem preoccupied with work and TV. To escape, both wives dabble with a Ouija board. The board spells out a name, Ezra, and implies that Mary Ellen will have an affair with that person.

Mary Ellen initially suspects her friend of manipulating the board and inventing its prediction. But for many of the forlorn characters in this collection, a thought quickly turns into an obsession. As the story focuses more on Mary Ellen, we see her days spent alone in movie theaters. At night, after drinking heavily, she drives to experience the rush of excitement, and to forget her paranoia that her husband is having an affair with Ivy. As "the needle was dancing between 105 and 110" (40), she dreams of Ezra, that shadowy figure that now lurks in her imagination, as her lover: "She gave herself briefly to the fantasy of this lone man . . . who approaches her stalled convertible, slowly, easily, reveling in his advantage" (32).

Herlihy has chosen an interesting name for this shadow. In the Old Testament, Ezra was a scribe that led the Jews from Babylon to Israel. In "A Story That Ends with a Scream," Ezra represents Mary Ellen's fantasy of escape from a life of tedium to one filled with sexual and personal completeness. The fact that Ezra means "God's Help" gives a spiritual undertone to Mary Ellen's search, its antiquated sound conflicting starkly with the contemporary experience of the trailer-park world. Such a conflict can also be understood with reference to the modern gothic, which offers, according to Carson McCullers, "a bold and outwardly callous juxtaposition of the tragic with the humorous, the immense with the trivial, the sacred with the bawdy, the whole soul of a man with a materialistic detail."[3] Thus Ezra takes on ironic connotations, resulting not in the salvation of Mary Ellen but in her tragic and desperate life becoming fused with the dark comedy of the moment.

On a night-time drive Mary Ellen is pulled over by a policeman who wears on his uniform the initial "E" of his first name. Convinced that this is the figure predicted by the Ouija board, she has sex on the beach with the policeman. But "E" stands for the Americanized name Eddie rather than the Hebrew Ezra, and the comedy of error signals her descent into physical and spiritual isolation. Returning confused and angry to the trailer park, she tries to strangle Ivy, whom she suspects of mischief as well as adultery with her husband. As Mary Ellen is guided home by her husband, her gaze becomes fixed on the night sky: "And there were all the stars to be confronted. They'd been waiting there to get at her eyes, millions of them waiting for millions of years, cool and utterly silent. Perhaps it was this silence in the sky that caused a new rush of panic." The brief but existential moment might suggest a turning point in the story when the protagonist becomes an individual "determined to make a real noise, one that would count for something" (47). That hope is brushed aside, though, and instead of letting out a scream, Mary Ellen is left to suffer in silence.

The next story in the collection, "Love and the Buffalo," reproduces the notes of an unnamed forty-six-year-old veteran of World War II who has been committed to a psychiatric hospital after breaking into the home of his ex-wife. The details of that marriage breakup are not given, but we are led to believe that it was a result of the mental breakdown of the narrator. Today we might diagnose this breakdown as post-traumatic stress disorder. In the midst of battle, he heard the ZZZ sound of an incoming missile. The explosion has left him with psychological injuries that have remained untreated. The character is haunted by the ZZZ sound and is convinced that it emanates from the very fabric of institutional life, from the continual buzz of the observation ward to the sound of the electric razor that the nurse uses to cut off his beard.

Like Ken Kesey's *One Flew over the Cuckoo's Nest* (1962), the story speaks to a generation surrounded by the so-called military-industrial complex and the genesis of the Vietnam War. The psychiatric hospital, with its gothic aura of confinement and illness, serves as a powerful metaphor for technological society and the individual struggling to survive within it. Billions of tranquillizers were prescribed during this period to calm the nerves of an increasingly anxious generation, but the narrator is also aware of their more sinister ramifications: "Tranquillizers subdue, mute, deaden, the caring centers in the brain. That's all there is to it. A tranquillizer is a lobotomy in pill form. Or to say it more accurately, it is a soporific for the soul. Zzzzz-zzzzz-zzzzz, sleeps the soul. While love [like the buffalo] dies" (61).

The physical and spiritual loneliness of the patient enables Herlihy to paint a picture of a world that lacks essential human feeling, dignity, and love. As the narrator says, "Has anyone, anywhere, ever postulated an even faintly valid reason for enduring a life from which love is gone forever? Is there anyone—I do not address myself to the dying, which includes of course the virtually millions of Z-puppets who clutter the world—is there anyone among the living few who knows a way to continue the labor of breathing without at least some small hope that love might one day be revived in him?" (64). As does Esther in Sylvia Plath's *The Bell Jar* (1963) or Billy Pilgrim in Kurt Vonnegut's *Slaughterhouse Five* (1969), the narrator of "Love and the Buffalo" contributes to a contemporary literary concern with the erosion of American standards of freedom and community. The narrator is clearly a very sick individual, whose paranoia of being transformed into a pill leads him to hide under his bed, where he is eventually discovered by the nurse, whom he imagines is named Miss Z.

"The Astral Body of a US Mail Truck" is also a first-person narrative, a suicide note perhaps, told under significant emotional pressure. The narrator,

Dorothy Fitzpatrick, is a forty-eight-year-old, childless widow whose husband, a fishing captain, was drowned at sea. Like many widows in Herlihy's short stories, Dorothy quickly becomes a "great reader in matters of metaphysics, astrology and spiritualism" (70). After a year of widowhood, she begins a relationship with Sidney Ritter—a nom de plume—her mailman. The daily sound of the mail truck causes Dorothy's heart to flutter, and Sidney is transformed from an ordinary mailman who lives with his mother and children into a "gallant horseman" (75). Are we meant to laugh at this exaggerated analogy? Certainly in a third-person narrative we would detect a sense of mockery of the characters and situation. But as Dorothy narrates the account, we are meant to understand that they are lonely people in search of companionship—a powerful theme in Herlihy's work.

As the relationship blossoms, Sidney's mother is taken into the hospital, and he is forced to take care of his children. As a result Sidney is able to meet Dorothy only during his breaks, which attracts an accusation from a neighbor, the malicious character Mrs. Malvina Cheney, that the couple is having sex on government time. The eventual showdown between these rival characters is described with particularly gothic wording: "It was hard to believe that such a nightmare was taking place right there on my own front porch in the rain. Sidney and I were both struck dumb with the horror of it." An uncontrollable emotion becomes evident in Dorothy's voice as she confronts her neighbor with an ultimatum: "'Malvina Cheney,' I said in a cold and frightening tone of voice. 'You remove yourself from my front porch this precise second, or I'll tear you in half'" (77). The character rises to the moment, but the situation is far from resolved.

Distressed at the confrontation, Sidney drives in the torrential rain, crashes the mail truck, and dies. Evident is Herlihy's interest in the complexity of characters' emotional reactions during trauma, as Dorothy laughs at the news of her lover's death. Following the death of her first husband, she believed that she acquired the gift of second sight. After Sidney's death she believes that she has become "sensitively attuned to the sound" both from the living and from the dead (80). Thus, like other stories in this collection, the lone narrator's tale is shaped by grief. Continuing to hear Sidney's mail truck, she is convinced "that anything sufficiently loved in the time of its life may achieve immortality in the astral plane." She adds a final note: "Upon further reconsideration, I see no reason whatsoever for sending a copy of this record to Mrs. Malvina Cheney" (81).

"The Day of the Seventh Fire" is set in Key West, cut off from the mainland during the hurricane season of the 1930s. Like the previous story, the narrative "casts back" into the past, this time in order to tell a tale "of revenge"

(86), the story of the two elderly unmarried Wilton sisters, Miss Erna and Miss Dolores. They are ladies of some wealth, having been left a considerable fortune and a large old house by their father, and therefore enjoy a certain status in the town. As with all the characters in this collection, the sisters have a certain eccentricity. This is especially true of Miss Dolores, who had once campaigned to lower the voting age to seven. Even her physical appearance seems grotesque, perhaps exposing the character's inner turmoil: "At seventy one she had eaten herself into the shape of a dumpling, but still she was a dashing thing to look at: painted her face, put bluing in her hair, and wore a black patch over her left eye. (No outsider knew for certain, but the patch was said to hide an enormous brown wart.)" (87). Miss Erna, the elder of the two, looks after her sister and tries to ensure that she stays out of trouble.

The problems seem to follow Miss Dolores's announcement of wanting to move out of the old house and into one of the sea-front cottages their father had left them. She claims to have had a premonition that something terrible would happen if they did not move. This premonition contributes to an unsettled feeling within the town, as there is an arsonist on the loose burning down homes and churches. When a twenty-year-old vagrant is caught trying to set alight the Cunningham home on Eaton Street, Miss Dolores shows a curious relationship toward him. She tells the arresting officer to "be gentle with him . . . and you may learn something about purity" (98). Here we see the combination of farce and tragedy. Certainly, at this point in the narrative, the reader is led to suspect that the younger sister has had a hand in the fires.

Life seems to settle into normality following the arrest of the arsonist, until one evening Miss Dolores, screaming, claims to have seen a stranger staring at her through the bedroom window. Leslie Fiedler sees the "shadow, the villain who pursues the maiden" as one of the most powerful of all the gothic symbols.[4] Although Miss Dolores is certainly no maiden, the stranger does have a significant presence in these stories, even if the shadowy malevolent aspect is often a figment of the central characters' exaggerated imaginations. As a result of the claim, each time Miss Dolores screams, the townsfolk come running to her aid. Even though Miss Erna suspects "that the peeper had been invented by Miss Dolores for the sole purpose of deviling her," she sits up every night with her father's shotgun hoping to catch the intruder (97). Eventually, after many long nights waiting, a stranger does appear, and in the panic Miss Erna is not able to shoot the gun, resorting instead to throwing the slop jar at the window. Suddenly the older sister is the center of attention in the local community, while Miss Dolores is unable to be found. She is eventually discovered hiding in the cinema, but while this has taken place, the old house has burned to the ground. Miss Dolores's reaction is odd; she thinks not of the burned-down home but of the new curtains that will be needed for their beach house.

What is the reader meant to understand in the peculiarities of this story, of its warped characters and burned-down old homes? In one sense the destruction of home represents a fracture between past and present. In *Renascence: Essays on Value in Literature,* Robert Phillips considers descriptions of decaying mansions as a metaphor for "disorder and insecurity and lack of moral center."[5] This metaphor patterns across the history of southern gothic writing, surfacing more recently in Cormac McCarthy's postapocalyptic novel *The Road* (2006). But Herlihy's characters are not shaped by profound circumstances. Rather, like the characters in O'Connor's "A Late Encounter with the Enemy" (1955), they are caught up in the triviality and absurdity of their own lives.

Like many of the stories in this collection, "Laughs, Etc" is preoccupied with death. The story is told by Gloria over the telephone to her friends Harry and Ceil. Set in New York's East Village, it deals with the effects of drug abuse on the period's youth. Gloria and Tom are survivors of drug abuse but still remain alcoholics in a barren relationship. They share a house with three junkies who live upstairs. These junkies are described as angels, perhaps as a reflection of the decade's idealism, and then as "young snotnoses," when, in reality, they demand money to feed their addiction for heroin (117). Herlihy's use of the grotesque relies on the juxtaposition between heavenly and human realms that make characters resemble the caricatures in Lyle Bongé's photographs of carnival parades.[6] As Gloria says, "I no more than hang up the phone when the parade begins. This lovely airborne parade. Angels and archangels. Cherubim and seraphim. All manner of winged creature, lighting gracefully on the furniture" (112).

Gloria's deep sense of guilt shapes these conflicting descriptions. As a result of her refusal to provide money for heroin, a girlfriend of one of the angels dies. This can be read, according to one reviewer, as "a crisp moment of defeat" for the characters, but there is also a wider mourning for the impending loss of the 1960s as a golden age.[7] One cannot ignore, though, that the girl was in a relationship with the "archangel," to whom Gloria has a particular sexual attraction. In that light the reason for denying her money for heroin takes on more selfish reasoning.

Thus grief and guilt imprison the narrator within a particular moment in the past. The title, "Laughs, Etc," relates to this moment, a party that took place in the house. Gloria invites people to the party: "dialing my fingies right down to the knuckles. *Come at once*! I shout to all and sundry; laughs, etc" (114). Here drugs and alcohol are readily available, and Gloria looks upon the three angels who live upstairs in both a sexual and paternal manner. Sitting outside on the fire escape, she hears one of the angels start to sing, to be joined by other young voices from the adjacent buildings. "It was as if we were all seven, and pure again," says Gloria, echoing the dream of Clinton Williams in *All Fall Down,* "and taking our first Holy Communion. Together. There was this feeling of the oneness of humanity" (119–20).

"The Fright of Mrs. Yeager" is set in a trailer park in West Palm Beach. Loretta Yeager has moved from Columbus, Ohio, so that her husband can enjoy his retirement. Outside the supermarket Ed, who is ten years older than Loretta, suffers a fatal heart attack, and she is "forced to turn her mind from the planning of a veal casserole to that of a funeral for the person with whom she's shared her life for the past fifteen years" (125). Like Dorothy's in "The Astral Body of a US Mail Truck," Loretta's grief is articulated in her withdrawal from the world. Despite protestations from her sister to return to Columbus, she remains in the trailer and develops a deep feeling of inferiority, seeing herself as a "lusterless, talentless woman at the ragged end of youth. With her grave empty eyes and no gifts whatever for traversing the deserts of solitude that seemed to lie before her" (135). The use of the word "seemed" to preface a sense of inferiority and weakness suggests that the feeling lies deep within the character's unconscious, something so visceral that it becomes a reality.

The two other characters in the story appear to function, at first, as catalysts for positive change in Loretta's attitude to life. But one of these characters, Mrs. Kay, turns out to be indifferent to her neighbor's grief and far too preoccupied with her own life and ego. Loretta's sister, Ida, wants her to return home to be with family. In a telephone conversation, Ida's reaction to her sister's tears shows a tendency for bullying, as well as other "unwholesome" meanings that linger below the surface of familial relationships in Herlihy's work: "Aaawww. Is my baby crying? Is it lonesome? Does it want to come back to C'umbus where it's loved?" (126, 133). In truth Loretta's individuality has always been constrained by a dominating sister and an argumentative husband, and now by a thoroughly objectionable old lady, Mrs. Kay.

According to O'Connor, "it is the extreme situation that best reveals what we are essentially."[8] The "fright," indicated in the story's title, is designed to expose Loretta to the lonesomeness of her life. In a daydream, for example, she reflects on the past: "Actually she couldn't even conjure up any clear image of him in her mind. It was as if the man who died had not been a person at all, but a faceless occupier of spaces" (127). But the fright eventually comes when Loretta wakes with a gasp in the early hours and notices the beginning of a letter to her sister that she had started in her sleep: "Dear Ida,

He knows I'm still here" (137). Those powerful words remind Loretta of the emptiness and artificiality of her life in the trailer park and highlight the necessity of escape to another place in order to learn to be her own person. This is both a problem and a solution dream, as Jayne D. Mack suggests, even though the latter is too ambiguous for such a weak character to act upon.[9] The story resists a happy ending, then, by having Mary Ellen utter the same platitudes to Mrs. Kay that have repressed and imprisoned her in the past.

"Terrible Jim Fitch" is a one-act play originally produced for the Off-Broadway stage. Set in a motel room in New Mexico, the play introduces us to the most psychopathic character in Herlihy's work. Brought up by his prostitute mother, a childhood spent moving from place to place, the title character has become, by his own admission, a "mental defective" who batters women and robs churches at gunpoint: "I got this *criminal mentality* where I enjoy being called a terrible person" (153). The other character in the room is Sally Wilkins. We know very little about her, as Fitch's violent behavior and alcohol-fueled speech intimidate her into total silence; her body, her only means of expression, is "all scrunched up hiding itself." We do know that she is a prostitute and "the personal and private property of one Jimmy K. Fitch," her pimp (148). In picturing a prostitute and her pimp, fugitives moving from city to city, state to state, hiding out in one cheap hotel room after another, we also see Fitch's adult life mirroring the transient experience of childhood with his mother.

Despite the physical realism of its set, the play does have a religious subtext. Fitch seems to be a character who steals from churches because he needs the money but also, perhaps more importantly, because he is angry with God, whom he imagines is a malevolent force in his life. Indeed, Fitch has a recurring dream in which people come together as a community seeking protection from the cruelty of God, and its detail reminds us of what Mack labels the golden-rope dream that patterns throughout Herlihy's fiction:

> Now, the dream: I dreamt I was sleeping not in any back seat, but in a great big mother-grabbing room, and in this room was every son-of-a-bitch in the world. I mean every man woman and child black white and yellow, and every wild tiger and every little puppy dog and every goddam grasshopper. That room had everything that's alive in it.
>
> And you know what we was doing? Me and all them Chinamen and old ladies and all them animals and kids and inseks, et cetera? We was in there praying together; eyes closed, setting still, and praying. Can you imagine that, Sal, me with my criminal mentality, having a dream about praying?
>
> Well, here's the twist; we wasn't praying to God, no, not by a damn sight! We was praying *about* Him. We was praying He wouldn't get us.

> Yea, you heard me. We was all in there, in this big room, and He was outside coming at us, God; and the way it was was: one at a time, He could take us—but if we stuck together, He couldn't, see? So all us live creatures was banded together in that room, safe. It was the sweetest damn dream. . . . get everybody to stick together and God will let up on you. (158–59)

As with the Misfit in O'Connor's "A Good Man Is Hard to Find" (1955), Fitch's pathology is driven by an existential relationship with God, even though his criminal history, in his eyes, makes him a "church man" (161). The play ends with no clear sign of what happens to them, although Fitch is growing increasingly frustrated at Sally's silence and smashes her ukulele against the wall. We are left to assume that the motel room becomes another one of Fitch's crime scenes.

"A Ceremony for the Midget" introduces us to Henry Rector and his wife Consilada, who have managed the Midget Bar and Grill in Key Bonita, Florida, for the previous twelve years. Of late, though, the number of customers has dwindled, resulting from Consilada's delusional belief that the midget of the bar's title actually exists. As a result of its reputation for violence, the bar has lost its drink license, and the bank has repossessed the property. Before they leave, a ceremony is organized to say goodbye to the place. The ceremony attracts only John and Patty, whose relationship began in the Midget, and the foursome sit in semidarkness around the bar. The "vigil," filled with silence and darkness, subtlely reveals the character's mental vulnerability, her "fragile expectancy in her mood that made each man feel he had been created for the express purpose of protecting her from disappointments" (173, 171).

As the ceremony ends with Henry throwing a crate of beer glasses into the mirror that hangs behind the bar, the story shifts between realism and a surreal world that has a leprechaun who suddenly appears on top of the piano. As the only other one in the otherwise empty bar, Consilada alone can see the leprechaun, which suggests that the story is playing on her unconscious. We know from earlier that a sense of the midget figure causes an interesting reaction in the character, "vigorously caressing her stomach as if to quiet the yowling of some anxious creature in her womb" (174). The mention of "womb" may suggest that the midget has represented a substitute for the child Consilada has so desperately craved.

The darkness and dilapidation of the bar are another gothic-inspired metaphor for the fragmentation of past and present, and also the tensions that hide within a person's emotional makeup. "A Ceremony for the Midget" has what all the other stories have: the removal of one of the key characters from a familiar world to an internal world of fantasy and horror. As Phillips says:

"The new Gothic novels are tales of tormented souls who view the world as a maze. The problems which confront them are complicated and terrifying as the twisted labyrinths of the Gothic castle. . . . The hero often is an individual who feels persecuted and inferior, and who withdraws from the actual world into a world of magnified fears and nightmares. This withdrawal results in a state of personal dissociation from society."[10] What has acted as a catalyst for Consilada's journey from one world to another is certainly the key mystery of this story, which could be unraveled by the reader by attending to her bitterness over a lack of children or her failure to be understood in marriage.

Juxtaposing midgets with "giants" is at the heart of the grotesque parade, which Herlihy reflects in the selection of these stories. "Sweet William" is set in Key West during the 1930s; it tells the story of William Bramer, a six-foot two-inch teenager whose significant physical presence calms screaming babies and rabid dogs. The story begins with the funeral of his father, Bull, who died in a bizarre gambling accident in a bar. We learn that Bull was a very cruel father, so it is no wonder that William smiles throughout the funeral service. The inheritance money allows mother, Miss Anna, and son to begin to live a comfortable life—"just the two of them, him and his beloved, plump little mama" (193).

As in all his work, Herlihy is not content just leaving this coziness intact. With the promise of earning one thousand dollars, Miss Anna accepts Mr. Bolts into her house and agrees to be his nurse and housekeeper before his imminent death. But Mr. Bolts refuses to die as expected, and what was "two's company" quickly becomes "three's a crowd." As it turns out, Mr. Bolts is a complainer and in constant need of Miss Anna's attention. As a result William acquires a "terrible new sadness," and his mother notices an increasing change in her son: "He was ordinary. . . . Her sweet William was nothing but a long, lanky lunk of a workman with his teeth going bad in front, signs of receding hair, lips that were dry and cracked and parted. . . . The William thing in him was absent" (202, 207).

There is something in the aura of Mr. Bolts that reminds William of the past, especially the past involving his father. As he looks at Mr. Bolts, or rather the shape of the person, he is reminded of some past mystery: "Somewhere in his memory was a similar thing, a thing of a like shape and character, and he racked his brain trying to remember what that long-ago thing had been. . . . William was unaccustomed to rummaging around in the bottom of his mind, looking for the faces of ugly lost things. It was like being in two places at once and all day long he kept going back and forth from where he was to where he wasn't" (195). That passage shows Herlihy's mastery of form, his ability to touch on a secret without revealing it to either the reader or, perhaps more importantly, the character who feels it. Often the characters in this collection never get to the answer or truth, and it is this failure that leads them to commit the bizarre actions they do.

In a desperate bid to get his old life back, William strangles Mr. Bolts to death. In an unusual ending, Miss Anna first, on finding the dead patient and realizing exactly what has occurred, calls the doctor to issue the death certificate. Two surprising things happen next. Before William is sent to be with friends for the afternoon, he passes his mother, "hurrying as if he'd been caged. As he passed her, Miss Anna did something that surprised her. . . . She spoke his name sharply, 'William!' He stopped walking, and before she knew what was happening, she'd slapped his face. Then she said, 'Oh, dear heaven!'" (211). Although Herlihy does not reveal the truth behind the tensions of each character—preferring what McCullers calls an "evocation of horror, beauty, and emotional ambivalence"—he does end his collection with a crystal-clear moral to the fable: do not put money before love.[11]

"Bad Bad Jo-Jo," dedicated to Herlihy's friend Joe Frazier, is set in Kaya Hathaway's penthouse overlooking Summit Place in New York.[12] Hathaway is the writer of the popular Bad Bad Jo-Jo books, which are "gory, campy melodramas" (70). The books have been made into movies, which have made Hathaway a camp icon of New York life, though also have made him suspicious of so-called friends, whom he believes are merely sycophants. The details of his apartment show an obsession with money, loneliness, fame, and ego: "*Prominent on one wall is a large lobby poster for a movie, Bad Bad Jo-Jo. Its illustration shows a little old lady with tiny eyeglasses and sensible shoes leading an enormous apelike young man by a chain. The young man wears an Uncle Sam hat that is too small for him*" (59). The penthouse has boxes everywhere, as Hathaway, overcome with paranoia that something bad is going to happen in America, is moving abroad. On the telephone Kayo tells his friend Roberta, "Something dreadful is going to happen here, and I don't want to be around when it does. . . . The stench of it is everywhere, it rises like fumes from the gratings in the streets, it lurks in doorways, it's the unwritten story on every front page" (61).

After two short opening scenes, one of which portrays Hathaway's nightmare, we are introduced to Frank Jones, a harmless-looking hack reporter who has come to interview his hero. The nightmare sets up an atmosphere of trepidation that invests the dialogue between the characters and the terrible events that are to unfold. Hathaway sees through the facade of this harmless reporter: "You're not just a fan. You're restless. Restless people always want something. And in your case, it's something specific" (69). That specificity is hinted at by Frank in one of the key turning points in the play:

FRANK: Now, about this terrific statement of personal philosophy—I have it right here—"You get what you give." Beautiful. I was just wondering if you ever worry about that, though. I mean, about getting what you give?

KAYO: Worry?

FRANK: Yes, sir. I mean, doesn't the idea ever bother you?

KAYO: What the hell are you talking about, does the idea ever *bother* me; it's made me rich and famous, you fool!

FRANK: Oh.

KAYO: Oh, what? You really are peculiar. I'd give a whole bagful of nickels to know what goes on in that head of yours.

FRANK (*straining after a thought*): You get what you give. See, I was thinking that if what you give to the world are these wonderfully campy murders, then maybe you'd be afraid that what the world would give back would be—well, the same thing!

KAYO: What in God's name does that mean?

FRANK: It's just—I wondered if you've ever been afraid of being—killed—in some wonderfully campy way? (71–72)

Hathaway enjoys the originality of this idea, but it also signals the introduction of Dennis, Frank's colleague. Where Frank plays docile, Dennis acts like a character up to no good. They ask Hathaway if they can show him their performance of Mama and Bad Bad Jo-Jo, who turn on their creator in a psychotic manner. After putting on raincoats to shield the duo against the blood, they murder Hathaway with a large knife. As Emerson said, in an extension of the collection's epigraph, "hideous dreams are exaggerations of the sins of the day." The play's reference to President Nixon suggests a political undercurrent, then, as Herlihy does not disguise the correlation between personal violence and the contemporary political context. The result is pure theatrical spectacle: "*The music of the nightmare is heard again now, and the lights are dimmed to black, as the two young men close in on* Kayo Hathaway. *The various stages of his murder, a deliberate, ritualistic event, are seen under the flashing lights of a stroboscope, while throughout the theatre and on the walls of the set, a rapid succession of photographic blow-ups is projected: a policeman clubs a peace marcher; a GI stabs a Vietcong; an 007-type shoots someone in the face; soldiers burn an Oriental village; someone is mugged; blacks smash a store window; a close-up of Sirhan Sirhan; President Nixon waves and smiles; Tommy Smothers looks bewildered; Allen Ginsberg prays*" (79).

A Story That Ends with a Scream and Eight Others explores the juxtaposition between surface reality and the hidden depths of characters' lives. These characters are often suspended between two worlds, one of the recent past and one of the uncertain present. They are defined by how they deal with that uncertainty, but in most cases they are unable to act in any meaningful way. The collection clearly demonstrates Herlihy's depth as a writer, and it attracted some positive reviews to that effect. On the whole, though, he felt dejected by the lack of critical attention accorded this collection. As his letters during the period show, he wanted to give up writing for good and be more fully part of the social world again. But not yet, for a great book had moved into his imagination.[13]

CHAPTER 7

The Season of the Witch

If James Leo Herlihy could have been granted a wish during the writing of *Midnight Cowboy,* it would have been to see America enter a golden age.[1] There seemed good reason to hope. A new countercultural generation believing in universal love had moved into Manhattan's East Village, where he kept a small apartment. In a decade that was quickly being engulfed by the Vietnam War, their long hair, flower-power fashion, and hippie vernacular represented an alternative lifestyle shaped by peace and spiritual harmony. Filled with optimism, Herlihy and his friend Evan Rhodes went on the road to search for further evidence of this generation. The journey lasted for six months and covered thirty-five thousand miles through California, Colorado, and New Mexico. What he found was astounding: thousands of young people living in communes, practicing free love, smoking marijuana, and organizing protests against the war.[2] The Beatles, the Rolling Stones, and Bob Dylan played their soundtracks. It seemed a revolution in embryo. *The Season of the Witch* (1971), which Tennessee Williams considered Herlihy's finest novel, grew out of that experience.[3]

In its themes *The Season of the Witch* echoes Herlihy's previous novels. The narrative is structured around the same rites of passage between adolescence and adulthood, a breakup of the traditional family, and a continuous interest in child-parent fixations. The difference is that seventeen-year-old Gloria Random, a name that suggests indirection, tells her own story throughout using notebooks. Undoubtedly, like Clinton Williams's notebooks in parts of *All Fall Down* (1960), this style enables the reader to gain a deeper insight into the character's emotional and psychological baggage. It is a first-person voice filled, like Huckleberry Finn's, with the innocence of youth, the spirit of adventure, and the vitality of a new beginning.

The novel touched a nerve. Its publisher Simon and Schuster sold out of its first print run of twenty-five thousand copies, helped, no doubt, by a Literary Guild recommendation. Herlihy received an unprecedented amount of mail from readers moved by Gloria's Holden Caulfield–like naivety. Perhaps they also saw a glimmer of Joe Buck in her bus journey from small-town Michigan to a life in New York. Accompanying her is her best friend and next door neighbor John McFadden, who is eluding conscription to the Vietnam War. Once in Greenwich Village, they become part of a household whose communal and experimental lifestyle serves to change Gloria's character in fundamental ways.

As much as the opening of *The Season of the Witch* sets up the conventions associated with a postwar road-trip genre, it is also an escape from both characters' parents. Gloria's mother, Irene, who resembles the neurotic Annabel Williams in *All Fall Down*, presides over the "dainty quilted prison" of suburban domesticity (12). Like Clinton, Gloria withdraws into notebooks, and she smokes marijuana to gain release from the phoniness of her mother's world. John's home is equally imprisoning. Unable to communicate with his psychoanalyst father and having heard rumors of his mother's suicide in an asylum, John withdraws to a life in the basement of the house. Always a haven in Herlihy's fictional world, the basement provides a near-private space for the development of both characters' friendship, their experimentation with drugs, and a secret understanding of John's homosexuality. Here they must have made plans to run away. For Gloria, this means the beginning of a quest for her real father, Hank Glyczwycz, a communist lecturer living somewhere in New York City, whom she has never met.

American literature is full of Greyhound buses crisscrossing the landscape, moving protagonists from one destination to the next. As Beat writers such as Jack Kerouac have shown, these journeys often symbolize a reclaiming of the frontier ethic of starting a new life. On route to New York, Gloria's change of name to Witch Glitz (an amalgam of Glyczwycz) and John's to Roy (short for Royal Prince) can in one respect be understood as the genesis of that quest to find oneself. They are, after all, "names that suit our souls" (29). However, Roy's reading of Herman Hesse's *Siddhartha* (1922) may offer another insight.

Although *Siddhartha* was first published in 1922, the interest in spirituality within it had an enormous impact on the countercultural movement of the 1960s. Its narrative follows a simple, though eloquent pattern. Siddhartha, in translation "he who has attained his goals," leaves an unfulfilling life in order to experience the world. Throughout the journey various encounters with characters serve to alter his sense of the world and his place in it. But one must be receptive to those encounters in order to understand the change taking place. That receptivity depends on a rejection of individual ambitions. Only then, as Siddhartha finds out, can a person be free. Gloria has to learn this lesson. Witch Glitz is a symbol of a quest to find her father and, in so doing, hurt her mother. Random, a name she quietly returns to at the end of the narrative, suggests the freedom of the soul born from indirection. Although the same message lies at the heart of Hesse's novel, it is also a quintessential American literary pilgrimage seen in works from Mark Twain's *The Adventures of Huckleberry Finn* (1884) to Jack Kerouac's *On the Road* (1957).

Gaining wisdom from encounters with other lives and societies is also Herlihy's means of developing his characters, of introducing them to experiences that will move them from childhood to a more mature understanding of their world. It could be said, then, that *The Season of the Witch* roughly follows the literary and philosophical principles of *Siddhartha.* The first such encounter Witch has on the bus is with her own unconscious. The reader is accustomed to Herlihy using dreams to penetrate the surface of his characters and expose their deeper feelings and emotions. As the bus approaches Philadelphia, for instance, Witch has a gothic nightmare of being a polluted Lake Erie. As the lake dies, Witch finds herself back in her own body but being chased by "a big black *thing* trying to catch us" (40).

Being chased by a dead lake can be translated as running away from the environmental impact of a postwar consumerism that her mother's life represents. But the "big black thing" can be read on other levels too. For a start, the nightmare represents Witch's unconscious as she tries to hide the fact that the journey was, in part, to hurt her mother. This is the painful child-parent relationship that haunts Herlihy's writing. Carl Jung, one of Herlihy's preferred theorists on human psychology, talks about a shadow hiding in unconscious as reflecting a collective anxiety.[4] Running away from the Vietnam War, from a society that Witch and Roy see as being clouded by an old-world conservatism, is very much a part of this. However, like the encounters in *Siddhartha,* the nightmare does not have to be understood as a wholly negative experience. By writing about it in her notebooks, Witch is in effect starting to deal with that experience. It would take almost two months of separation from that old life, though, for her to learn the wisdom to bring this anxiety to some kind of resolution.

As Joe Buck discovers, New York is no Land of Oz. Witch's first encounter with the city leads her to document its pollution, noise, and foul smells. As both characters walk through various neighborhoods searching for a cheap hotel, they witness an environment blighted by prostitution, child begging, and heroin addiction. Witch, though, is still too naive to understand the significance of these sights. Once in a hotel, she defends prostitution as "a perfectly splendid profession" (66). After receiving a slap across the face and threats of further violence from a neighbor who happens to be a prostitute, Witch is shocked into a realization of their different economic and social worlds. Roy is given a similar experience from a drug dealer who, knife to throat, takes all his money in return for nothing. From both encounters they have learned a painful, yet important lesson: cities, like jungles, are dangerous places. Herlihy, however, wrote *The Season of the Witch* to "suggest a philosophical approach that would be useful . . . rather than reviewing the pain."[5] The characters' introduction to the "Canal Street Experimental Station en route to Utopia" is certainly an important part of that philosophy (106).

Both Siddhartha and Joe Buck learn that to enter another society, one needs a guide. Sally Sunflower, unlike Rico Rizzo in nearly every respect, represents the bridge between what Witch calls "the dark ages of my girlhood" and a new life (12). Sally is a fascinating figure, "one of the first flower children" and a true pioneer of the 1960s. She is certainly one of Herlihy's most actively political female characters, whose daily life is shaped by faith in a "post-revolutionary economy. . . . You do what you can for others, and when you need something for yourself, you ask for it" (86). Like Herlihy, she took part in the numerous political protests against the Vietnam War, which included the now-famous attempt in October 1967 to exorcise President Lyndon Johnson from the White House. It is her existential practice of doing, rather than talking about it, and her reluctance to take hard drugs to get high that make her an example of the possibilities envisaged by the youth movement.

As both a guide and model of the youth revolution, Sally introduces a key dream to the novel. It is a dream that a reader of Herlihy's work will be familiar with: "Sally said, 'Okay, let's close our eyes together.' We closed our eyes and sat in silence for a minute. 'I see this fabulous light, don't you?' she said. I hadn't, but I began to, and it seemed to grow stronger. Roy said he saw it, too. Sally said, 'You know what the light is?' Roy said, 'I'm not sure. What is it?' 'That's us and it's especially strong because there's three of us. And we're together!' We said wow. Sally said, 'Think how it will be when the whole world's together!'" (91).

An echo of Clinton Williams's recurring dream of the world in an apple orchard or Joe Buck's similar golden-rope dream, Sally's shared vision reflects the human need for companionship. But this companionship is not part of a traditional family structure. During this period Herlihy was convinced that the "human family doesn't work anymore. People seem to know that it doesn't fit anymore, that it doesn't have to."[6] Rather, Sally speaks from experience and leads Witch and Roy into an alternative form of life practiced in the Canal Street home.

As in the Williams home in *All Fall Down* or the X flats in *Midnight Cowboy,* there is something "special" about the gothic nature of the "haunted ramshackle house" in the "spooky" and dimly lit neighborhood of Canal Street (73). Herlihy's writing is certainly full of grotesque characters, their lives twisted by the emotional and psychological baggage that drags them down. But the "family of freaks" (166) whom Witch and Roy meet see themselves as pioneers of alternative ways of living. For all their idealism, the family is based on American principles of freedom, equality, and happiness of the individual. The young dropouts live cooperatively under the guidance of Peter Friedman, the pun saying a lot about his character. He is a former psychoanalyst, and his partner Doris is a former Hollywood talent agent. One cannot help but see Herlihy in aspects of Peter's character. Lyle Bongé, for instance, in a heartfelt obituary, remembered his friend's devotion to giving sanctuary to young dropouts escaping the commercialism of society or the Vietnam War.[7]

Yet Peter is not introduced to the reader straightaway, on account of his being in California caring for his dying father. In his absence Witch pieces together "little sketches of others" (100). In one respect these sketches, perhaps unconsciously, situate characters in particular categories. These categories could be given the following labels: intellectual; calming; parental. The reader should bear in mind, though, that these are not rigid categories, as characters can belong to more than one, but they do aid an understanding of the novel's structure.

Take Neyeurme, or Nyoom for short, and Jeanette. Both African Americans, they are depicted as two of the family's most intelligent members. A thirty-year-old New York cab driver, self-educated Nyoom is a voracious reader, deep intellectual thinker, and eloquent defender of the Black Panthers. His vision of the future, though, borders on the apocalyptic. Despite the rest of the world existing in peace, he pictures an America caught up in corruption and greed, heading for atomic annihilation. It is intriguing to wonder whether such visions mask Nyoom's personal insecurity, but Witch, after all a teenager writing for herself, never provides enough detail about the character's background to enable the reader to make any kind of judgment. Jeanette, on the other hand, has had a distinguished academic education. A graduate in modern foreign languages, she uses her skill to earn money from translation work, contributes regularly to the family's "Grocery Pig," and helps keep the house in order (96). Like Sally Sunflower, she is the epitome of Anaïs Nin's model of a fulfilled person.[8] For Herlihy, that philosophy ought to be the basis of any revolution.

The cooperative and personal philosophy also extends to an understanding of Cary Colorado (named by his mother after Cary Grant). Despite his apelike appearance, on the surface a feature of the grotesque, Cary represents a pure form of love and absolute devotion to communal living. As a teacher of yoga, his presence has a calming influence on the group, especially later in the narrative where there is a tense discussion between Hank and Peter. Cary's experimentation with getting high without drugs and his use of meditation lead to the characters' spiritual contemplation of themselves as individuals and part of a community.

Peter and Doris, as the oldest members of the family, have adopted, perhaps unconsciously, a parental role. Their wise counsel offers guidance without judgment to most of the family members. This is particularly significant for Witch, who treats Peter almost like a surrogate father while she contemplates her relationship with her real father. His absolute faith in the revolutionary potential of the young and his genius for political insight makes him one of the most respected members of the family. The death of his father takes this insight to a new level: "He said one of the great differences between the new age and the past would be that, from now on, children would inherit more and more light from their parents, and less and less darkness. We'll learn to be aware, we'll learn to watch ourselves in such a way that when the ghosts of our parents show themselves in our behavior we'll be free to pick and choose. We'll take what's wise and beautiful, and be happy that it's a part of us, and we'll simply reject what's ugly and dark" (218). Witch will remember Peter as one of "my beautiful teachers" (362). Although Witch does not fully realize it, those sentiments represent a key moment in that education that, by the end of the novel, allows her to return home to Michigan as her own person.

Rejecting "what's ugly and dark" is one of the key challenges of Herlihy's characters. Jayne D. Mack may be on to something in her belief that Witch's quest for her father "is also a troubling metaphor that represents each character's quest for private certainties."[9] This is certainly true of Peter. As he returns from California to Canal Street, he finds strangers waiting to purchase drugs from another member of the house, Archie Fiesta. Although Archie is one of Herlihy's most handsome characters, he is also, internally, one of his most damaged. What we see in Archie throughout the novel is not development but regression into a state of complete dependency on heroin. Finding Archie's stash of drugs, Peter violently evicts him from the house. But Peter's guilt is immediate. He realizes that despite Archie's breaking the rules of the home, he has behaved as his parents would have done. And that, for Peter, is a microcosm, even a justification, of America's involvement in Vietnam.

Peter seems to realize that revolutions taking steps forward are in constant danger of taking steps back. For all their idealism, the Canal Street family can unintentionally reproduce the social conventions of the past, especially concerning traditional gender roles. Not far removed from the depiction of the Major in *Blue Denim* (1958), the male characters appear to have a monopoly on political debate. When female characters do contribute, for example Doris, it is to ask questions of the male characters, while admitting "I'm just not terribly political" (298). As Witch realizes, though, Doris is "mother's age and came out of the same bullshit" (176). There are fewer excuses for Jeanette, who seems to prefer tidying the house, sewing, and embroidery to any political engagement. Perhaps such stereotypes represent a flaw in the novel or its realism. Doris may have the final word on this issue, as it crosses into Herlihy's conviction: "This is a whole new age we're heading into, and nobody but *nobody* knows what it's going to be. All we can do is dream and try and hope and flounder" (181–82).

For all the characters' flaws and insecurities, the commune helps to build an atmosphere of mutual respect. Roy, for instance, has never seen such love between people. Their everyday use of drugs, such as marijuana, enables them to explore the possibilities of themselves as spiritual and political beings and helps them to see their lives as a microcosm of how things could be. A new version of the golden-rope dream shapes Peter's personal vision of the future: "Every man, woman, and child on the planet earth will form its own chain of hands. . . . Just as we do here at the table each night" (275). A postnational world, where human brotherhood ends the validity of institutions, cannot be taught but only lived each day and learned by example.

Witch, exposed to that life, is certainly learning. The longer she stays in the household, the more her notebook entries appear to reflect an understanding of the information being imparted to an imagined reader. At the time of writing, the reader must be herself, so we are able to see the notebook not only as a reflection of her day-to-day existence but also as a guide to her future life. On one occasion, for instance, and with writer's block, she decides to copy down a selection of quotations written on the family's notice board. These include mottos such as "If you love one person, yourself, you can love the world" and "Be yourself: No one can ever tell you you're doing it wrong," which underpin the family's daily rituals and Witch's growing sense of maturity and wisdom. Perhaps this is best seen in her inclusion of Walt Whitman's sentiments: "I hear and behold God in every object, yet I understand God not in the least / Nor do I understand who there can be more wonderful than myself" (153, 155, 158).

Herlihy toyed with the idea of using a part of Whitman's poem "Song of Myself" (1855) as the novel's epigraph.[10] Certainly it can be understood, along with the golden-rope dream, as one of the novel's key statements. The quotation again helps to illuminate the "Canal Street Experimental Station en route to Utopia" as an American phenomenon, a Manifest Destiny perhaps of the liberty and happiness of the individual as a microcosm of the whole.

Although Herlihy believed the 1960s to be "the first drug generation,"[11] an age when Timothy Leary called on the young to "turn on, tune in, drop out,"[12] he did not think that *The Season of the Witch* was a novel preoccupied with drugs. There is, though, in its pages discrimination between drugs that enlighten and drugs that damage. Certainly marijuana, a drug that Herlihy took most of his life, is seen to enlighten both consciousness and conversation. For Gloria and Roy, marijuana helps them escape the old world of their parents and see the world with fresh eyes. But members of the commune also experiment with ways of getting high without the use of drugs. Indeed, as Doris says: "Each of us feels marijuana has helped him become a better person. . . . But the whole point of smoking is to use less and less, not more and more" (264). As if to offset the commune's romanticism of drugs, there emerges a fleeting glimpse of another, less-glamorous world where drugs ruin lives. Both Witch and Roy become painfully aware of this other world as they search for Archie Fiesta at his last known address: "The whole place was a shambles. The kitchen window was wide open and the wind was blowing in, tearing at the window shade. Most of the furniture was upside down and broken. The mattress had been slashed open. The stuffing was coming out and there was blood all over it, dozens of big dried spots. . . . And probably, for the rest of my life whenever I think of Archie, I'll see his beautiful face in my mind and I'll hear that window shade flapping, flapping, flapping" (347). Archie has become one of the period's anonymous statistics concerning rates of addiction. His disappearance, for Herlihy, represents the sadness and loneliness endemic to urban life, and he makes his narrator aware of this for the rest of her life.

The juxtaposition of those worlds—one visionary, one blighted by the reality of drug addiction, another caught up in the baggage of the past—shapes Witch's complex relationship with her father. She enters the life of Hank Gliss (another name change from Glyczwycz) masquerading as a student rather than his love child of a fleeting relationship with Irene. This distance allows the reader to understand Hank, like Archie, as a damaged person. Sacked from "three universities for preaching Communism" (125), despised by his current students, and divorced from his wife and children, he is surely one of Herlihy's most bitter characters. His withdrawal to an isolated, run-down farmhouse on Staten Island symbolizes the extent to which cynicism has replaced the deep political beliefs that he originally brought to America as a refugee from war-torn Europe. After Witch invites him for dinner at the Canal Street home, the reader sees just how much Hank symbolizes a past that threatens to hold back the optimism of a contemporary youth revolution.

At the dinner table Hank criticizes and ridicules the naivety of the group's political vision. On the surface the episode can be understood as a simple conflict between optimism and pessimism, the young and the old. As Herlihy must have realized, the latter has the potential to win such a debate because it lacks any political idealism and is armed with evidence of the horrors of history. In one of the most insightful observations into another character, Witch realizes how the complexity of the past controls Hank's thinking: "His life had taught him to land the first blow, to strike before he was struck. He'd never been into peace. He'd lived in a world of attack and retaliation" (284). Absolute belief in such grand concepts as peace and universal brotherhood is therefore severely unsettled by Hank, forcing Peter to arrive at a more pared-down philosophy that reflects the very nature of Herlihy's writing: "A Man alone isn't much. In twos he may improve somewhat" (304). Interestingly what Witch learns from this episode is not the vulnerability of Canal Street but a genuine sympathy for her mother that she will carry when she eventually returns home.

Although *The Season of the Witch* is undoubtedly Herlihy's most political book, it retains the same urge to explore characters' emotional and sexual lives that has featured prominently in all of his writing. Here teenage sex, male prostitution, and homosexuality are represented in order to unsettle conservative attitudes and to show readers the nature of a society on their doorsteps. However, as we have seen, perhaps the most controversial issue broached by Herlihy in his work relates to unusual relationships, a fixation haunted by sexual undertones between mother and son. Herlihy, a lover of sexual freedom, wanted that taboo smashed: "So many of our tensions and anxieties are a result of this awful dread of sexuality between parent and child. If your first physical relationship . . . is fraught with taboo and restriction, then the pattern of inhibition is set."[13]

Whether this view enables us to reread the causes of Joe Buck's naivety in *Midnight Cowboy* is debatable. *All Fall Down,* though, toys with the fixation between Berry-Berry and his mother, Annabel, and Shirley calls Clinton by her dead brother's name, Willy, before having sex. Similarly in *The Season of the Witch,* Edward, who acts camp in order to attract women, refers to Witch as his sister before they have sex.

Perhaps Herlihy does occupy the voice of Peter here, as he realizes that the hang-ups of the past, however controversial and upsetting, have to be addressed for any revolution to succeed. At the same time, though, the psychoanalyst in him makes him aware of the damage that such a relationship could inflict on a person's mental state. It is, to borrow the words of Anthony Burgess's *MF* (1971; a novel that also dealt with incestuous relationships), "the irresponsible cultivation of chaos."[14] Whether chaos has a positive or a negative energy is the question.

Peter's thoughts do not arrive out of the blue. They are in response to Witch's speaking to him about her decision to begin a sexual relationship with her father. Like Herlihy, Peter would have been versed in the writings of Jung and his belief that incestuous relationships are symbolic attempts to regain a lost world of childhood and domestic security.[15] Hank, of course, remains ignorant of the fact that the young woman he wants to sleep with is actually his daughter. When he does find out, because Witch tells him, the effect is catastrophic. Although the reader is party to the full aftereffects of this revelation, it would be an almost sure bet that Hank slips further into the withdrawal and bitterness that have, since his arrival in America, marked his life.

Although Herlihy was a passionate believer in the youth movement, he remained concerned about its future in the contemporary city. His answer—"to evacuate the cities"—shapes the development of his last two novels.[16] In this light we can understand the journey that some of the commune's members make from New York to Canada. This is triggered by Roy's increasing anxiety over being arrested by the police for his AWOL status. But as much as this is an escape from the American city, it also reclaims the frontier ethic of journeying to the New World. Herlihy was not on his own in considering this option for his characters. Perhaps Ken Kesey in the most famous novel of the decade, *One Flew over the Cuckoo's Nest,* also envisaged Canada as a new start for his protagonists Randolph Patrick McMurphy and Chief Bromden. Witch's decision to leave New York is abrupt, perhaps reflecting Roy's panic about being caught, but the utopian possibility of their destination does not let them down. As in the first glimpses of the New World, Witch sees Canada's enormous sky, underneath which "there's plenty of peace, space, time, air, freedom, everything a person could want" (351).

But there is something amiss, of course. Witch's growing maturity has made her aware that "If there's suffering in America . . . I'm part of what's caused it" (351). With that wisdom she decides to return to New York, which ends up as a return home to Belle Woods, Michigan, and her mother. Herlihy's works, with the exception of his short-story collections, continuously move his characters toward some kind of resolution. Having spent only two months away from home, Witch has crossed the psychological boundary that separates adolescence and adulthood, and she has acquired the wisdom to listen and the confidence to act on her own judgments.

As she hitches her way home, the reader is introduced to her final encounter, who offers her a ride. Mr. Kaminski, a middle-aged man who has just returned from visiting his daughter in a psychiatric hospital, represents a barometer of the character's transformation. To assuage Mr. Kaminski's guilt over the state of his daughter, for instance, Witch tells him, "I didn't believe it was fair to lay all the hangups on one's parents" (361). This advice is as relevant to her as it is to her new friend, and it is illustrative of the unconscious strength she is now drawing on. As much as Mr. Kaminski is a listener, he is also Witch's final teacher, who enables her to see the reality of her journey: "Periods and the young need such periods, he said, and perhaps cutting myself off from my mother for a while, cruel or not, was the healthiest thing I could have done" (363).

Mr. Kaminski helps the reader to understand how Witch's journey to New York was in essence a pilgrimage for self-realization that enables her to relate to her mother on new terms. Finding Irene overwhelmed with her own problems—her husband has left her for a younger woman, causing her irrationally to have a face-lift—Witch has a new role: to comfort and reassure. Their relationship is now based on mutual respect for each other as people rather than on obligations. As a result each forms a silent pact "to allow each other to be" (375). This seems to be the end of the name Witch and the birth of someone entirely new. Like Huck Finn, she cannot settle in her mother's domestic world and knows, as if instinctively, that it will soon be time to move on. The revolution has happened, as Sally Sunflower predicted, and it has given to the world one fulfilled person.[17]

In an interview with *Gay Weekly,* Herlihy admitted that *The Season of the Witch* "was more or less dated by the time the ink dried."[18] Although the expectation of universal peace and brotherhood was diluted by the onset of a new decade, the late 1960s had represented a growing political awareness in Herlihy that he wanted invested in his work. More than that, the period showed him how to live. Like Witch, he felt himself a fulfilled person now and no longer wanted to spend eight hours a day locked in his study writing fiction. He wanted to be with and among people.[19] Witch's remark "I've been overdoing it, so I decided all writing must be some kind of sickness," then, signaled the end of Herlihy's literary career and the commencement of a new life (244).

NOTES

Chapter 1—Understanding James Leo Herlihy

1. Bonetti, "Interview with James Leo Herlihy" (audiocassette).

2. See Stanley, "Interview with James Leo Herlihy." In the preamble to the interview, Stanley says that Herlihy's "overseas orders were dated 12 August 1945, but the war ended on the 14th" (18).

3. "Obituary of James Leo Herlihy," *Daily Telegraph*, 28 October 1993, 23.

4. Annie Albers as quoted in Katz, *Black Mountain College*, 31. Albers taught printmaking at the college between 1933 and 1949. Numerous books offer an informative understanding of the college as well as Albers's life in the institution with her husband Josef. I have found the best of these to include Martin Duberman, *Black Mountain: An Experiment in Community* (1972; reprint, Evanston, Ill.: Northwestern University Press, 2009); and Mary Emma Harris, *The Arts at Black Mountain College* (Cambridge, Mass.: MIT Press, 1987). Further resources can be found on the following Web site: http://www.bmcproject.org/Resources/resources.htm (accessed 9 June 2011).

5. Harris, "Interview with James Leo Herlihy," 1.

6. Ibid., 27.

7. See Bongé, *Sleep of Reason*. The book includes Herlihy's interview of Bongé.

8. See James Leo Herlihy Papers, 1959–86, University of Delaware Special Collections.

9. Harris, "Interview with James Leo Herlihy," 36, 38. There is some confusion about the length of Nin's stay at the college. Herlihy says she stayed for three days, though Deirdre Bair's biography of Nin claims four days. I have gone with the latter claim. See Deirdre Bair, *Anaïs Nin: A Biography* (New York: G. P. Putnam's Sons, 1995), 330.

10. Nin, *Diary*, 5:98.

11. Herlihy, "Art of Being a Person," 67.

12. See Harris, "Interview with James Leo Herlihy," 158.

13. *Streetlight Sonata* was performed on 3 June 1950. The quotation is taken from the theater program. See James Leo Herlihy Collection, Howard Gotlieb Archival Research Center, Boston University. *Moon in Capricorn* was directed by Miranda d' Ancona and Audrey Hilliard and performed at Theatre De Lys, New York, on 27 October 1953. Both plays remain unpublished.

14. In an interview Herlihy claimed to have had "about forty-five of those little jobs, altogether," but after the success of *Blue Denim* on Broadway, "No more dishwashing" (quoted in Newquist, *Conversations*, 135).

15. Noble had also written a number of plays, including *Starfish* (1952). The play was also produced for Kraft Television Theatre, NBC, on 27 June 1956.

16. Herlihy was keen to point out that *All Fall Down* was not actually his first novel. He had written a number of novels that "will remain unpublished" (quoted in "James Leo Herlihy," *Current Biography,* 33).

17. Mack, "Dream Motif in the Novels of James Leo Herlihy," 2.

18. See Herlihy's introduction to Stephen Arnold's *Epiphanies,* n.p.

19. Herlihy as quoted in Bailey, introduction to *Midnight Cowboy,* [1965, 1–8,] 4.

20. Herlihy to M. C. Richards, 19 June 1970, in James Leo Herlihy Papers.

21. See Bonetti, "Interview with James Leo Herlihy." She did surprise him in the interview, though, with her view that his previous books have a powerful political sensibility. As Herlihy responded: "Well, I didn't notice that."

22. Ibid.

23. Nin, *Diary,* 5:53.

24. "J. L. Herlihy: *Midnight Cowboy* Author," *Los Angeles Times,* 28 October 1993, http://articles.latimes.com/1993-10-23/news/mn-48680_1_midnight-cowboy (accessed 25 May 2011).

25. Ibid.

26. James Leo Herlihy, *Season of the Witch* (London: W. H. Allen, 1971), 218. It is the aptly named character Peter Friedman who utters these profound words in the novel.

27. Herlihy to Richards, 27 August 1980, James Leo Herlihy Papers. The letter continues: "I want to help the students get in touch with their own motives, help them find connections between their writing ambitions and the kind of lives they'd like to make."

28. Bongé, "Obituary of James Leo Herlihy."

29. At the time of writing this introduction, Herlihy's work is largely ignored in critical studies. Still, there are scholars currently devoted to reversing this neglect. For example, Michael Snyder has recently completed a Ph.D. dissertation titled "Mixed-blood Metaphors: Allegories of Native America in the Fiction of James Purdy," which makes significant comparative references to Herlihy's writing. He is now working on a critical biography of Herlihy. See his informative essay "James Leo Herlihy and Key West." The piece is accompanied by Bud Lee's excellent photographs of Herlihy in Key West.

30. Herlihy to Richards, 30 October 1973, James Leo Herlihy Papers.

31. Herlihy to Richards, 18 February 1974, James Leo Herlihy Papers.

32. Herlihy played a role in Arthur Penn's film *Four Friends* (1981). He also acted in Robert Parrish's movie *In the French Style* (1963).

33. Nin refers to these "black withdrawn moods" in her *Diary,* 5:126. On her first visit to Black Mountain, Nin remembered a conversation with Herlihy about "a chart he kept in his journal. It was designed like a fever chart, only instead of fever it recorded the ups and downs of his moods. . . . Jim said, pointing to the chart: 'The day it goes below this point I will commit suicide.'" See Stuhlmann, "From Jim to Jamie," 120–21.

34. Herlihy to Lyle Bongé, 11 August 1989, James Leo Herlihy Papers.

35. Bongé, "Obituary of James Leo Herlihy."

36. For further information on Herlihy's view of the period as a golden age, see Martha Macgregor, "The Week in Books," *New York Post,* 24 April 1971, n.p.

Chapter 2—*Blue Denim*

1. Nin, *Diary,* 5:197. See also "James Leo Herlihy." *Current Biography,* 31–33. Here we learn that "Herlihy has been a farm hand, picnic-plate wrapper, soda-dispenser, foil for a carnival medicine man, snake exhibitor, actor, director, grocery and drugstore clerk, bellboy, bookseller, purchasing agent, editor, and inspector of guided missile instruments" (31).

2. Herlihy, *Blue Denim;* quotations from this volume are hereafter cited parenthetically within the text.

3. Brooks Atkinson, "Blue Denim," *New York Times,* 20 April 1958, sec. 2, 1.

4. This is the last time that Detroit was represented as a significant location in Herlihy's work. It is almost as if the city of his birth and growing up had to be dealt with before moving on to the more familiar settings of Florida and New York that permeate his writing.

5. Elaine Tyler May, *Homeward Bound: American Families in the Cold War* (New York: Basic Books, 1988), 14.

6. James Leo Herlihy Collection.

7. Allyn, *Make Love Not War,* 38.

8. Bonetti, "Interview with James Leo Herlihy."

9. May, *Homeward Bound,* 153.

10. Rickie Solinger, "Pregnancy and Power before Roe and Wade, 1950–1970," in *Abortion Wars: A Half Century of Struggle, 1950–2000,* ed. Rickie Solinger (Berkeley: University of California Press, 1998), 27.

11. Indeed in early drafts Herlihy referred to the play as "The Children's Comedy" (James Leo Herlihy Collection).

12. Atkinson, "Blue Denim," 17.

13. John Gassner "American Crisis?," in *Best American Plays: Fifth Series 1957–1963,* edited by John Gassner (New York: Crown, 1963), xiv.

14. David Savran, *Communists, Cowboys, and Queers: The Politics of Masculinity in the Work of Arthur Miller and Tennessee Williams* (Minneapolis: University of Minnesota Press, 1992), 36.

15. Robert Vorlicky, *Act Like a Man: Challenging Masculinities in American Drama* (Ann Arbor: University of Michigan Press, 1995), 15.

16. Douglas T. Miller and Marian Nowark, *The Fifties: The Way We Really Were* (Garden City, N.Y.: Doubleday, 1977), 285.

17. I have borrowed these revealing words from Savran, *Communists, Cowboys, and Queers,* 9.

18. Atkinson, "Blue Denim," 1.

19. Thomas P. Adler, *American Drama, 1940–1960: A Critical History* (New York: Twayne, 1994), 5.

20. C. W. E. Bigsby, *Modern American Drama, 1945–2000* (Cambridge: Cambridge University Press, 2000), 34.

21. Robert Lowell from his poem "Memories of West Street and Lepke," in Lowell, *Life Studies* (1959; reprint, New York: Farrar, Straus & Giroux, 2007), 90.

Chapter 3—*The Sleep of Baby Filbertson and Other Stories*

1. Nin, *Diary,* 5:118. At the same time Nin was worried that her friend's work was also hampered by the limits of realism and his overriding concern for misfits: "Letter

to Jim: This is a difficult letter to write and I hope you will bear with me. Because I love you so deeply I cannot lie to you. . . . From the beginning, you remember, we had a discussion about you putting yourself inside of little people. . . . Why, why, I wondered, must we put such emotional experiences of complex feelings in such characters?" Herlihy's response was blunt: "You even say that there are kinds of human beings, 'limited, inarticulate, shrunken, dwarfed,' who are not worth writing about. Can you mean it? Is there such a thing on earth as a human being of so little value that he is outside of a writer's focus? Did I misunderstand you?" (5:218–19).

2. James Leo Herlihy, *The Sleep of Baby Filbertson and Other Stories* (1959; Harmondsworth: Penguin, 1964); quotations from the 1964 volume are hereafter cited parenthetically within the text.

3. Nin, *Diary,* 6:168.

4. The story was also adapted to the stage by Herlihy, with significant changes, under the title *Crazy October: A Comedy.* He toured the country with it, premiering in New Haven, Connecticut, on 8 October 1958 and closing in San Francisco on 3 January 1959. The play was partially successful, due in no small part to Tallulah Bankhead's role as Daisy Filbertson, but its grotesque humor often confused the audience. As Bankhead said, "It rather baffles the audience. . . . I think in Europe it would be a success. They dig that kind of thing." For further information on this tour, see Lobenthal, *Tallulah!,* 481–82.

5. Carl Jung as quoted in Anaïs Nin, *The Diary of Anaïs Nin: Vol. 1, 1931–34,* edited by Gunther Stuhlmann (Boston: Houghton Mifflin Harcourt, 1966), 132.

6. The length of the story may be a result of Herlihy's intention that it be a novel. Interestingly Herlihy also wrote the story as a play, which he titled "A Breeze from China." See James Leo Herlihy Collection.

7. Bailey, "Interview with James Leo Herlihy," 21.

8. Nin, *Diary,* 5:253.

9. I refer to Nin's collection of stories *Cities of the Interior* (Athens, Ohio: Swallow Press, 1959).

10. James Leo Herlihy Collection.

Chapter 4—*All Fall Down*

1. James Leo Herlihy, *All Fall Down* (1960; reprint, Harmondsworth: Penguin, 1962); quotations from the 1962 edition are hereafter cited parenthetically within the text.

2. Nin, *Diary,* 6:62.

3. Ibid., 221.

4. Bonetti, "Interview with James Leo Herlihy."

5. Irving Malin, *New American Gothic* (Carbondale: Southern Illinois University Press, 1962), 56. Malin is speaking specifically about the gothic sensibility of Truman Capote.

6. Arthur Miller, *Death of a Salesman* (1949; reprint, New York: Viking Press, 1955), 132, 114. For more details of Miller's idea of literary tragedy, see his essay "Tragedy and the Common Man" (1949), http://vccslitonline.cc.va.us/tragedy/miller essay.htm (accessed 2 June 2011).

7. Herlihy, introduction to Bongé, *Sleep of Reason,* 14.

Chapter 5—*Midnight Cowboy*

1. James Leo Herlihy, *Midnight Cowboy* (1965; London: Scribner, 2003); quotations from the 2003 volume are hereafter cited parenthetically within the text.

2. James Herlihy to M. C. Richards, n.d., James Leo Herlihy Papers, 1959–86.

3. See Mack, "Dream Motif in the Novels of James Leo Herlihy."

4. Herlihy as quoted in Newquist, *Conversations,* 138.

5. The idea that Joe Buck's path to New York and his friendship with Rico are somehow fated is alluded to throughout the narrative. As Joe boards a bus to Houston, for instance, a woman sings a song about "a *wheel of fortune turning turning turning,*" and listening, he realizes that "he had no words for destiny" (11). It is interesting too that Townsend P. Locke sees his life as a grotesque trick of fate as "he was *supposed to die in the war!* But he didn't. There was some idiot mistake in heaven, and he's still here" (217).

6. See Ward, "I'm Walking Here!"

7. I use the word "Whitmanite" carefully, especially because of the poet's democratic inclusion of all Americans in his work. Joe Buck's interest in "the sight of other men at their labor" (151) is thus similar to Whitman's poem "A Song of Occupations" in *Leaves of Grass* (1855). Jeffrey Bailey goes further with this connection: "Herlihy belongs to a distinguished line of American writers who may be termed 'native' because their artistic sustenance depends upon their native and physical environment. Through his perception of life as the poetry of being and his use of language less as explication than as a vehicle to express the continuum of emotion, he is a *de facto* heir of the tradition of Walt Whitman, Hart Crane, Sinclair Lewis and Tennessee Williams. Having been spawned by the contemporary American scene, Herlihy's work flows and returns to the same source: the consciousness that defines and nurtures the national entity. In many ways, he is the prototype of that writer, peculiar to the American tableau, who functions outside a literary establishment or hierarchy, and whose work becomes a mirror of the communal soul; he is a writer who captures from his own experience a significant and abiding moment in the experience of his race." See Bailey, introduction to *Midnight Cowboy,* [1965, 1–8], 3.

8. Jane Jacobs, *The Death and Life of Great American Cities* (1961; reprint, New York: Modern Library, 1993), 6. For another interesting viewpoint on Moses, see Marshall Berman, *All That Is Solid Melts into Air: The Experience of Modernity* (London: Verso, 1983).

9. Lyle Bongé to James Herlihy, James Leo Herlihy Papers.

10. Saylor, "Orpheus in New York," 82.

11. Although outside the scope of this book, there is certainly a case to be made for comparing the novels of James Purdy with Herlihy's work. Purdy's statement on his own writing, for instance, could easily be applied to a reading of *Midnight Cowboy:* "My writing is both realistic and symbolic. The outer texture is realistic, but the actual story has a symbolic, almost mythic quality. The characters are being moved by forces, which they don't understand. . . . Though my stories are really American myths and the language and characters are very American" (James Purdy Society Web site, http://www.wright.edu/~martin.kich/PurdySoc/Artistic%20Statement.htm [accessed 24 May 2011]). For further comparisons between these two writers, see Snyder, "Mixedblood Metaphors."

12. Terrell Dixon as quoted in Mack, "Dream Motif in the Novels of James Leo Herlihy," 72n2.

13. For an alternative view of Joe Buck's fate, see Mitzel, "Interview with James Leo Herlihy." Here, Herlihy offered a pessimistic view of Joe Buck's life after the closing scene: "Joe Buck was no hustler; he was too soft a touch himself ever to succeed in exploiting others. What became of him? The story is too sad to tell. My days of making people cry have, I hope, come to an end" (8).

14. I refer to Auden's poem "September 1st, 1939" (1939). The poem can be read on the following Web site: http://www.poets.org/viewmedia.php/prmMID/15545 (accessed 10 June 2011).

15. These words are taken from Herlihy's "Untitled Essay," in *Sexual Latitude: For & Against,* edited by Harold H. Hart, 12. The full quotation reads as follows: "Cities everywhere are becoming uninhabitable, suffocating under blankets of smog and garbage."

16. Ibid., 17.

Chapter 6—*A Story That Ends with a Scream and Eight Others*

1. James Leo Herlihy, *A Story That Ends with a Scream and Eight Others* (London: Jonathan Cape, 1968), 7; quotations from this volume are hereafter cited parenthetically within the text. The epigraph to the collection is taken from Ralph Waldo Emerson's essay "Spiritual Laws" (1841). The following paragraph, taken from that essay, may be helpful for understanding Herlihy's purpose: "Our dreams are the sequel of our waking knowledge. The visions of the night bear some proportion to the visions of the day. Hideous dreams are exaggerations of the sins of the day. We see our evil affections embodied in bad physiognomies. On the Alps, the traveller sometimes beholds his own shadow magnified to a giant, so that every gesture of his hand is terrific. 'My children,' said an old man to his boys scared by a figure in the dark entry, 'my children, you will never see any thing worse than yourselves.' As in dreams, so in the scarcely less fluid events of the world, every man sees himself in colossal, without knowing that it is himself. The good, compared to the evil which he sees, is as his own good to his own evil. Every quality of his mind is magnified in some one acquaintance, and every emotion of his heart in some one" (*American Transcendentalism Web,* http://www.vcu.edu/engweb/transcendentalism/authors/emerson/essays/spirituallaws.html [accessed 24 May 2011]).

2. Bernard Bergonzi, "Not Long Enough," *New York Review,* 9 November 1967, 33.

3. Carson McCullers, "The Russian Realists and Southern Literature," in *The Mortgaged Heart,* edited by Margarita G. Smith (1941; reprint, Boston: Houghton Mifflin, 2005), 252–53.

4. Leslie A. Fiedler, *Love and Death in the American Novel* (1960; reprint, London: Dalkey Archive, 1998), 132.

5. Robert S. Phillips, "The Gothic Architecture of *The Member of the Wedding,*" *Renascence: Essays on Values in Literature* 16, no. 2 (Winter 1964): 60.

6. See Bongé, *Sleep of Reason.*

7. Bergonzi, "Not Long Enough," 34.

8. Flannery O'Connor, *Mystery and Manners: Occasional Prose,* edited by Robert Fitzgerald (New York: Farrar, Strauss, Giroux, 1969), 113.

9. See Mack, "Dream Motif in the Novels of James Leo Herlihy," 2.

10. Phillips, "Gothic Architecture of *The Member of the Wedding,*" n.p.

11. McCullers, "Russian Realists and Southern Literature," 252. Here, McCullers is referring specifically to the work of William Faulkner.

12. "Bad Bad Jo-Jo" does not appear in *The Story That Ends with a Scream* but rather in Herlihy's collection of three short plays, *Stop, You're Killing Me* (1970). I include it here because it appeared in that volume alongside "Laughs, Etc" and "Terrible Jim Fitch." Quotations from "Bad Bad Jo-Jo" are hereafter cited parenthetically in the text.

13. These closing words are informed by Herlihy's particular process of writing, which he referred to in an interview about *Midnight Cowboy:* "There is a mystery involved in the writing process—there's a compulsiveness about it. . . . For me, I know that a book has to be written when one character, one specific being, has moved into my head and unpacked and doesn't show any sign of leaving" (Herlihy as quoted in Bailey, introduction to *Midnight Cowboy,* [1965, 1–8], 4).

Chapter 7—*The Season of the Witch*

1. See Martha Macgregor, "The Week in Books," *New York Post,* 24 April 1971, n.p.

2. See "J. L. Herlihy: *Midnight Cowboy* Author," *Los Angeles Times,* 28 October 1993, http://articles.latimes.com/1993–10–23/news/mn-48680_1_midnight-cowboy (accessed 25 May 2011).

3. James Leo Herlihy, *The Season of the Witch* (London: W. H. Allen, 1971); quotations from this volume are hereafter cited parenthetically within the text.

4. See Carl G. Jung, *The Portable Jung,* edited by Joseph Campbell (Harmondsworth: Penguin, 1976).

5. Bonetti, "Interview with James Leo Herlihy."

6. Herlihy as quoted in F. K. Plous Jr., "Herlihy Sees a Flowering Youth," *Chicago Tribune,* 26 April 1971, 2. For further examination of the golden-rope dream, see Mack, "Dream Motif in the Novels of James Leo Herlihy."

7. See Bongé, "Obituary of James Leo Herlihy."

8. See Herlihy, "Art of Being a Person," 67.

9. Mack, "Dream Motif in the Novels of James Leo Herlihy," 75.

10. See earlier drafts of the novel in James Leo Herlihy Papers, 1959–86.

11. Herlihy as quoted in Cleveland Amory, "Tradewinds," *Saturday Review,* 20 May 1971, 10.

12. See Timothy Leary, *Turn On, Tune In, Drop Out* (1965; reprint, Oakland, Calif.: Ronin, 1999).

13. Herlihy as quoted in Bailey, "Interview with James Leo Herlihy," 22.

14. Anthony Burgess, *MF* (1971; reprint, Harmondsworth: Penguin, 2004), 200.

15. See especially Jung, "Individual Dream Symbolism in Relation to Alchemy," in *Portable Jung,* 323–455.

16. Joe O'Sullivan, "From Cowboy to Woodstock Wonderland," *Sunday Star* (Washington, D.C.), 8 May 1971, B5.

17. See Herlihy, "Art of Being a Person," 67. Here he refers to Nin's desire to "contribute to the world one fulfilled person—myself."

18. Herlihy as quoted in Mitzel, "Interview with James Leo Herlihy," 7.

19. Amory, "Tradewinds," 10.

BIBLIOGRAPHY

Primary Sources

BOOKS BY JAMES LEO HERLIHY

Although first editions are cited here, in some cases
later editions are cited in the endnotes.

Blue Denim. New York: Random House, 1958.

The Sleep of Baby Filbertson and Other Stories. New York: E. P. Dutton, 1959. The collection was also published in 1970 as *Crazy October* (New York: Lancer).

All Fall Down. New York: E. P. Dutton, 1960.

Midnight Cowboy. New York: Simon & Schuster, 1965.

A Story That Ends with a Scream and Eight Others. New York: Simon & Schuster, 1967.

Stop, You're Killing Me. New York: Simon & Schuster, 1970.

The Season of the Witch. New York: Simon & Schuster, 1971.

SELECTED NONFICTION WRITING BY JAMES LEO HERLIHY

"Broadway: Little Theatre Show Business." *Center: A Magazine of the Performing Arts* 1 (September 1954): 12–15.

"Untitled Essay." In *Sexual Latitude: For and Against,* edited by Harold H. Hart, 10–21. New York: Hart, 1971.

Introduction to *The Sleep of Reason: Lyle Bongé's Ultimate Ash-Hauling Mardi-Gras Photographs,* by Lyle Bongé, 7–14. Highlands, N.C.: Jargon Society, 1974.

"The Art of Being a Person." *Anaïs: An International Journal* 1 (July 1983): 67–68.

Introduction to *Epiphanies,* by Stephen Arnold, n.p. Pasadena, Calif.: Twelvetrees Press, 1987.

UNPUBLISHED WORKS BY JAMES LEO HERLIHY

The following unpublished manuscripts are held in the James Leo Herlihy
Collection, Howard Gotlieb Archival Research Center, Boston University.

Plays

"Telephone Portrait of Scotty and His Three Women" (1950).

Streetlight Sonata: A Modern Tragedy. The play, directed by Philip Van Dyke and John Landreth, was first performed at the Playbox, Pasadena Playhouse, 3 June 1950.

Moon in Capricorn. The play, directed by Miranda d' Ancona and Audrey Hilliard, was first performed at Theatre De Lys, New York, 27 October 1953.

"The Black Nun," with William Noble (1955).

"The Giant and the Ragpicker" (1956).

Crazy October: A Comedy. The play premiered in New Haven, Connecticut, on 8 October 1958 and closed in San Francisco on 3 January 1959.

"Time to Kill: A Comedy," with James Kirkwood (n.d.).

"A Breeze from China" (n.d.)

Novels

"The Witch Bride" (1951).

"Strangers from Home" (1952).

"Patience-on-the-Mickmack, Ohio" (1961).

"The Witch Bride" (1965).

Motion Pictures with Appearances by James Leo Herlihy

In the French Style. Directed by Robert Parrish. Written by Irwin Shaw. Starring Jean Seberg, Stanley Baker, Philippe Forquet, Addison Powell, and James Leo Herlihy. Columbia Pictures, 1963.

Four Friends. Directed by Arthur Penn. Written by Steve Tesich. Starring Craig Wasson, Jodi Thelen, Michael Huddleston, Jim Metzler, and James Leo Herlihy. Orion Pictures, 1981.

Motion Pictures and Television Adaptations of James Leo Herlihy's Works

Box 704. Directed by Richard Dunlap. Written by James Leo Herlihy. Starring Betsy Meade and Paul Carr. Kraft Television Theatre, NBC. 1956.

Blue Denim. Directed by Philip Dunne. Written by Philip Dunne and Edith R. Sommer. Starring Carol Lynley, Brandon de Wilde, Macdonald Carey, Marsha Hunt, and Warren Berlinger. 20th Century Fox. 1959.

All Fall Down. Directed by John Frankenheimer. Written by William Inge. Starring Eva Marie Saint, Warren Beatty, Karl Malden, Angela Lansbury, and Brandon de Wilde. Warner Brothers. 1962.

Midnight Cowboy. Directed by John Schlesinger. Written by Waldo Salt. Starring Dustin Hoffman, John Voight, Sylvia Miles, John McGiver, and Ruth White. MGM. 1969.

Terrible Jim Fitch. Directed by James Ferman. Written by James Leo Herlihy. Starring Nicol Williamson and Marianne Faithful. Thirty Minute Theatre, BBC. 1971.

Secondary Sources

BOOKS, ARTICLES, AND INTERVIEWS

Allyn, David. *Make Love Not War: The Sexual Revolution; An Unfettered History.* Boston: Little, Brown, 2000.

Bailey, Jeffrey. "Interview with James Leo Herlihy." *Advocate* no. 191 (25 August 1976): 21–23.

———. Introduction to *Midnight Cowboy.* 1965; reprint, New York: ibooks, 2002, 1–8.

Bair, Deirdre. *Anaïs Nin: A Biography.* New York: G. P. Putnam's Sons, 1995.

Barrios, Richard. *Screened Out: Playing Gay in Hollywood from Edison to Stonewall.* New York: Routledge, 2003.

Bonetti, Kay. "Interview with James Leo Herlihy." April 1982. Columbia, Mo.: American Audio Prose Library, 1982 [audiocassette].

Bongé, Lyle. "Obituary of James Leo Herlihy." *Independent* (London), 29 October 1993, 16.

———. *The Sleep of Reason: Lyle Bongé's Ultimate Ash-Hauling Mardi-Gras Photographs*. Highlands, N.C.: Jargon Society, 1974.

Bordman, Gerald. *American Theatre: A Chronicle of Comedy and Drama*. Vol. 3: *1930–1969*. Oxford: Oxford University Press, 1996.

Bowles, Paul. *In Touch: The Letters of Paul Bowles*. New York: Farrar, Straus & Giroux, 1994.

Broughton, James. *Coming Unbuttoned*. San Francisco: City Lights, 1993.

Cromie, Robert. *James Leo Herlihy Discusses* A Story That Ends with a Scream (audiocassette). Authors and Their Books. Tucson Motivational Programming. 1969.

Finstead, Suzanne. *Warren Beatty: A Private Man*. London: Random House, 2006.

Griffith, Benjamin W. "Midnight Cowboys and Edwardian Narrators: James Leo Herlihy's Contrasting Voices." *Notes on Contemporary Literature* 2, no. 2 (1972): 6–7.

Harris, Mary. "Interview with James Leo Herlihy." November 1972. North Carolina Museum of Art, Raleigh.

Harrison, Gilbert A. *The Enthusiast: The Life of Thornton Wilder*. New Haven, Conn.: Ticknor & Fields, 1983.

Highwater, Jamake. *Shadow Show: An Autobiographical Insinuation*. New York: Alfred Van Der Marck Editions, 1986.

Isherwood, Christopher. *Diaries*. Vol. 1: 1939–60. London: Methuen, 1996.

Jackson, Joe. "Gigolos: The Last of the Courtly Lovers." *Journal of Popular Culture* 15 (Fall 1981): 130–41.

"James Leo Herlihy." *Current Biography: Who's News and Why* 22, no. 1 (1961): 31–33.

Katz, Vincent E. *Black Mountain College: Experiment in Art*. Cambridge, Mass.: MIT Press, 2003.

Kaufelt, Lynn Mitsuko. *Key West Writers and Their Houses*. Englewood, Fla.: Pineapple Press, 1986.

Kendle, Burton S. "James Leo Herlihy." In *Contemporary American Dramatists*, edited by K. A. Berney, 261–65. London: St. James Press, 1994.

Lobenthal, Joel. *Tallulah! The Life and Times of a Leading Lady*. London: Aurum Press, 2005.

Mack, Jayne D. "The Dream Motif in the Novels of James Leo Herlihy." Master's thesis, University of Houston, 1975.

Mitzel, John. "Interview with James Leo Herlihy." *Gay Weekly*, 25 September 1976, 8–9.

Morritz, Charles. *Current Biography: Who's News and Why*. New York: H. W. Wilson Company, 1961.

Newquist, Roy. *Conversations*. Chicago: Rand McNally, 1967.

Nin, Anaïs. *The Diary of Anaïs Nin*. Edited by Gunther Stuhlmann. Vol. 5: 1947–55. London: Peter Owen, 1974. Vol. 6: 1955–66. London: Peter Owen, 1977. Vol. 7: 1966–74. London: Peter Owen, 1980.

Pervy, C. D. "Songs of Innocence and Experience: Herlihy's *Midnight Cowboy*." *Forum* 13 (Winter 1976): 62–67.

Picano, Felice. *True Stories: Portraits from My Past*. New York: Chelsea Station Editions, 2011.

Price, Julia S. *The Off-Broadway Theatre*. New York: Scarecrow Press, 1962.

Richards, Stanley, ed. *The Best Short Plays*. New York: Chilton Books, 1971.

Riley Fitch, Noël. *The Erotic Life of Anaïs Nin*. London: Abacus, 1994.

Saylor, Charles F. "Orpheus in New York: The Classical Descent of *Midnight Cowboy*." *Classical Bulletin* 46, no. 6 (1970): 81–84, 95.

Sherrill, Roland A. *Road Book America: Contemporary Culture and the New Picaresque*, 215–27. Urbana: University of Illinois Press, 2000.

Simmons, David. "The Countercultural Cowboy: Rereading the 1960s Novels of Doctorow, Herlihy, and Portis in a Marcusian Framework." In *Westerns: Paperback Novels and Movies from Hollywood*, edited by Paul Varner, 215–27. Newcastle upon Tyne: Cambridge Scholars, 2007.

Snyder, Michael. "James Leo Herlihy and Key West." *Littoral: The Journal of the Key West Literary Seminar*, 29 April 2010. http://www.kwls.org/littoral/james_leo_herlihythe_midnight/ (accessed 6 June 2011).

———. "Mixedblood Metaphors: Allegories of Native America in the Fiction of James Purdy." Ph.D. diss., University of Oklahoma, 2009.

Stanley, Richard. "Interview with James Leo Herlihy." *In Touch* 28 (March 1977): 18–19, 87, 90–91.

Stuhlmann, Gunther. "From Jim to Jamie: Tracing a Friendship in Anaïs Nin's Diary." *Anaïs: An International Journal* 11, no. 12 (1994): 120–24.

Unrue, Darlene Harbour. "Selected Letters from a Writer's Life." *Mississippi Quarterly* 49 (Winter 1995): 119–27.

Ward, Robert. "'I'm Walking Here! I'm Walking Here!': New York Flâneurs in James Leo Herlihy's *Midnight Cowboy*." In *The Idea of the City*, edited by Joan Fitzpatrick, 159–68. Cambridge: Cambridge Scholars, 2009.

Wilder, Gilbert A. Harrison. *The Enthusiast: The Life of Thornton Wilder*. New Haven, Conn.: Ticknor & Fields, 1983.

Williams, Tennessee. *Where I Live: Selected Essays*. Edited by Christine R. Day and Bob Woods. New York: A New Direction Book, 1978.

ARCHIVES

George Freedley Papers, New York Public Library. http://www.nypl.org/archives/4358 (accessed 9 June 2011). Mainly letters.

Jamake Highwater Papers, 1954–2001. New York Public Library. http://www.nypl.org/archives/1432 (accessed 9 June 2011). Mainly letters.

James Leo Herlihy Collection, Howard Gotlieb Archival Research Center, Boston University. http://www.bu.edu/phpbin/archives-cc/app/details.php?id=7939 (accessed 9 June 2011). Extensive resources.

James Leo Herlihy Papers, University of Delaware Special Collections, http://www.lib.udel.edu/ud/spec/findaids/herlihy.htm (accessed 9 June 2011). Extensive resources.

Noël Riley Fitch Papers, Harry Ransom Center, University of Texas at Austin. http://research.hrc.utexas.edu:8080/hrcxtf/view?docId=ead/00196.xml (accessed 9 June 2011). Mainly letters.

INDEX